CONFIGURING PROCUREMENT AND SOURCING WITHIN DYNAMICS AX 2012

BY MURRAY FIFE

© 2015 Blind Squirrel Publishing, LLC, All Rights
www.dynamicsaxcompanions.com

ISBN-10: 1512021970

ISBN-13: 978-1512021974

Preface

What You Need For This Guide

All the examples shown in this blueprint were done with the Microsoft Dynamics AX 2012 virtual machine image that was downloaded from the Microsoft Customer Source or Partner Source site. If you don't have your own installation of Microsoft Dynamics AX 2012, you can also use the images found on the Microsoft Learning Download Center or deployed through Lifecycle Services. The following list of software from the virtual image was leveraged within this guide:

*   Microsoft Dynamics AX 2012 R3

Even though all the preceding software was used during the development and testing of the recipes in this book, they may also work on earlier versions of the software with minor tweaks and adjustments, and should also work on later versions without any changes.

Errata

Although we have taken every care to ensure the accuracy of our content, mistakes do happen. If you find a mistake in one of our books—maybe a mistake in the text or the code—we would be grateful if you would report this to us. By doing so, you can save other readers from frustration and help us improve subsequent versions of this book. If you find any errata, please report them by emailing editor@blindsquirrelpublishing.com.

Piracy

Piracy of copyright material on the Internet is an ongoing problem across all media. If you come across any illegal copies of our works, in any form, on the Internet, please provide us with the location address or website name immediately so that we can pursue a remedy.

Please contact us at legal@blindsquirrelpublishing.com with a link to the suspected pirated material.

We appreciate your help in protecting our authors, and our ability to bring you valuable content.

Questions

You can contact us at help@blindsquirrelpublishing.com if you are having a problem with any aspect of the book, and we will do our best to address it.

Table Of Contents

www.dynamicsaxcompanions.com

INTRODUCTION

The Procurement and Sourcing area within Dynamics AX not only allows you to manage and track all of the purchasing activities within your organization. It is also where you can manage all of your purchasing hierarchies, which allow you to organize all of your purchased products into more manageable groups. You can initiate purchase orders, manage the changes to the purchase orders, and even raise requisitions that can then work through approval workflows before you convert them into live purchase orders. All of these transactions then feed down into the Accounts Payable module, making the whole procurement cycle seamless.

Setting up the Procurement and Sourcing details are not hard either and this guide is designed to give you step by step instructions to show you how to configure the Purchasing area, and also how some of the basic parts work to get you up and running.

INTRODUCTION

The Procurement and Sourcing area within Dynamics AX not only allows you to manage and track all of the purchasing activities within your organization. It is also where you can manage all of your purchasing hierarchies, which allow you to organize all of your purchased products into more manageable groups. You can initiate purchase orders, manage the changes to the purchase orders, and even raise requisitions that can then work through approval workflows before you convert them into live purchase orders. All of these transactions then feed down into the Accounts Payable module, making the whole procurement cycle seamless.

Setting up the Procurement and Sourcing details are not hard either and this guide is designed to give you step by step instructions to show you how to configure the Purchasing area, and also how some of the basic parts work to get you up and running.

CONFIGURING PROCUREMENT & SOURCING CONTROLS

Before we start though there are a couple of codes and controls that we may want to set up within the Procurement & Sourcing area which will make the system work just a little better.

Configuring Buyer Groups

The first set of codes that we will configure within the Procurement & Sourcing area will be the **Buyer Groups**. These will be used later on to segregate out our products into different buying groups that can then be used to group our purchase orders for review and approval.

Configuring Buyer Groups

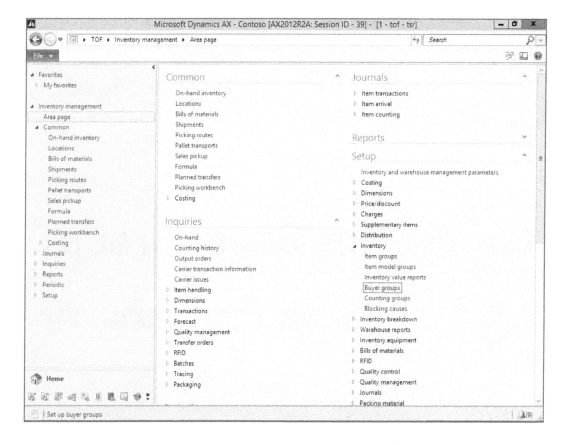

To do this, click on the **Buyer Groups** menu item within the **Inventory** folder of the **Setup** group within the **Inventory Management** area page.

Configuring Buyer Groups

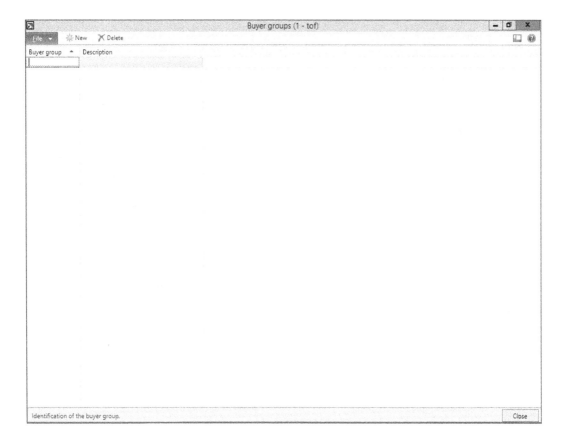

When the **Buyer Groups** maintenance form is displayed, click on the **New** button in the menu bar to create a new record.

Configuring Buyer Groups

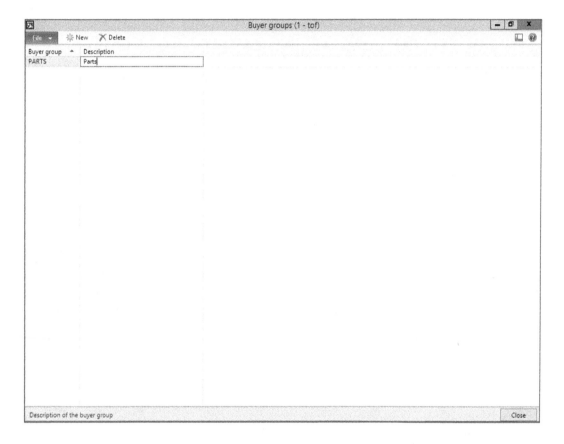

Then set the **Buyer Group** code to **PARTS** and the **Description** to **Parts.**

Configuring Buyer Groups

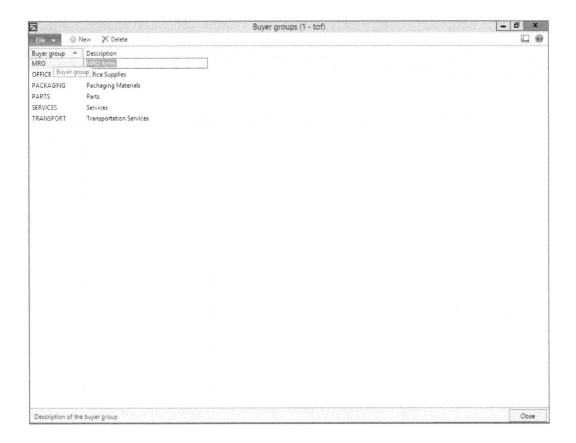

Repeat the process by adding in a few more **Buyer Groups**

Buyer Group	Description
SERVICES	Service
TRANSPORT	Transportation Services
PACKAGING	Packaging Materials
OFFICE	Office Supplies
MRO	MRO Items

When you done, just click on the **Close** button to exit from the form.

Configuring Delivery Terms

Next we will configure a few **Delivery Terms** codes that we will be able to use within our Purchase Orders.

We will configure some of the common **Incoterms**. For more information on these click here:
http://en.wikipedia.org/wiki/Incoterms#EXW_.E2.80.93_Ex_Works_.28named_place.29

Configuring Delivery Terms

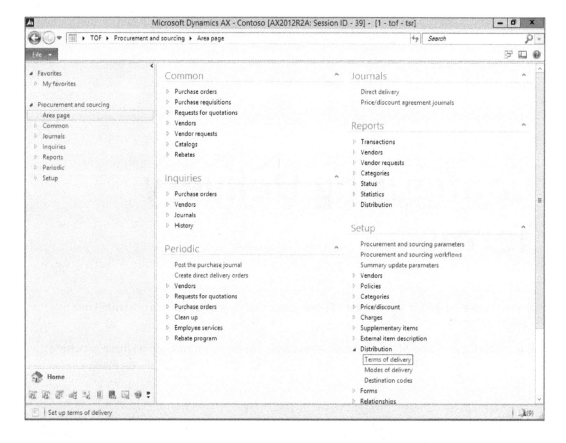

To do this, click on the **Terms Of Delivery** menu item within the **Distribution** folder of the **Setup** group within the **Procurement and Sourcing** area page.

Configuring Delivery Terms

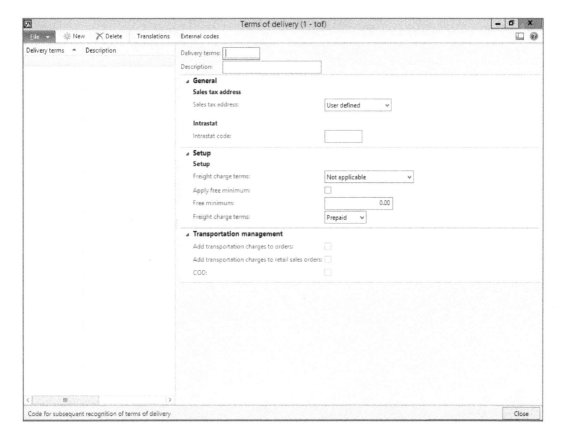

When the **Terms of Delivery** maintenance form is displayed, click on the **New** button in the menu bar to create a new record.

Configuring Delivery Terms

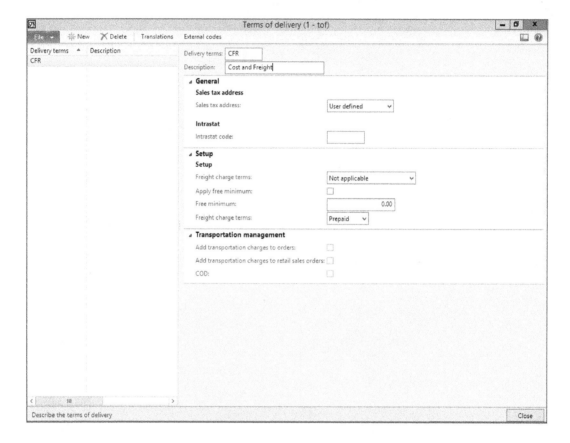

Then set the **Delivery Terms** code to **CFR** and the **Description** to **Cost and Freight**.

Configuring Delivery Terms

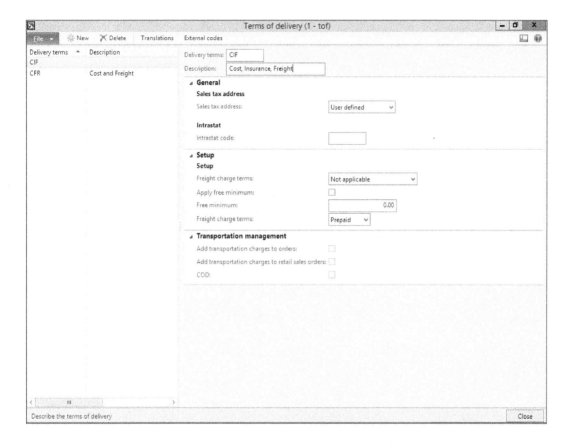

Click on the New button to add another record and then set the **Delivery Terms** code to **CIF** and the **Description** to **Cost, Insurance, Freight**.

Configuring Delivery Terms

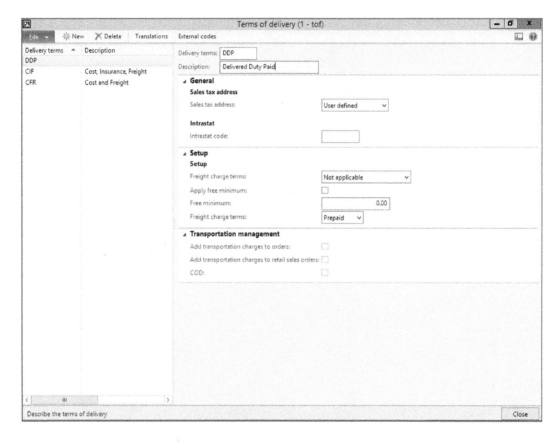

Click on the New button again to add another record and then set the **Delivery Terms** code to **DDP** and the **Description** to **Delivered Duty Paid**.

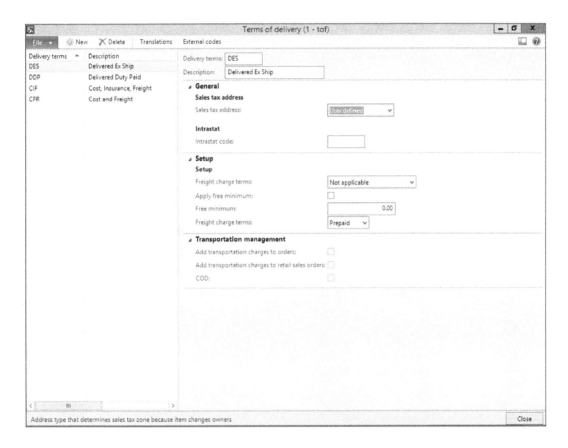

Click on the New button again to add another record and then set the **Delivery Terms** code to
DEX and the **Description** to **Delivery Ex Ship**.

Configuring Delivery Terms

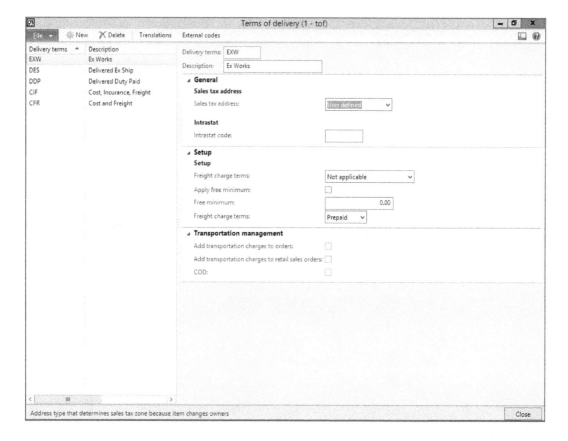

Click on the New button again to add another record and then set the **Delivery Terms** code to **EXW** and the **Description** to **Ex Works**.

Configuring Delivery Terms

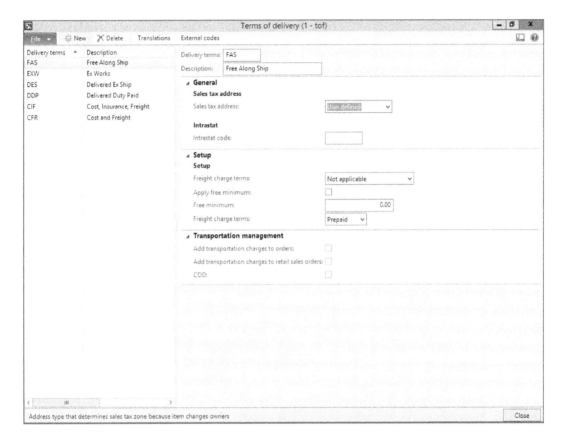

Click on the New button again to add another record and then set the **Delivery Terms** code to **FAS** and the **Description** to **Free Along Ship**.

Configuring Delivery Terms

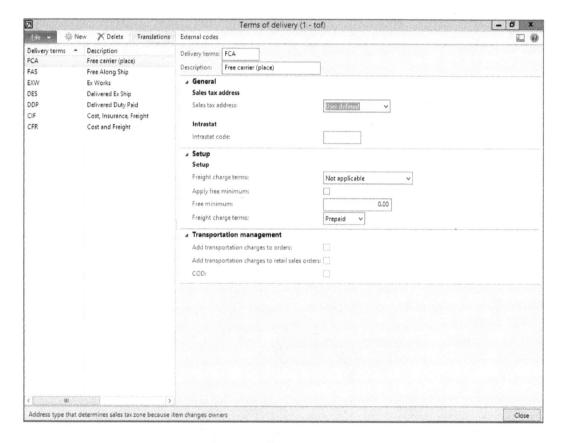

Click on the New button again to add another record and then set the **Delivery Terms** code to **FCA** and the **Description** to **Free Carrier (Place).**

Configuring Delivery Terms

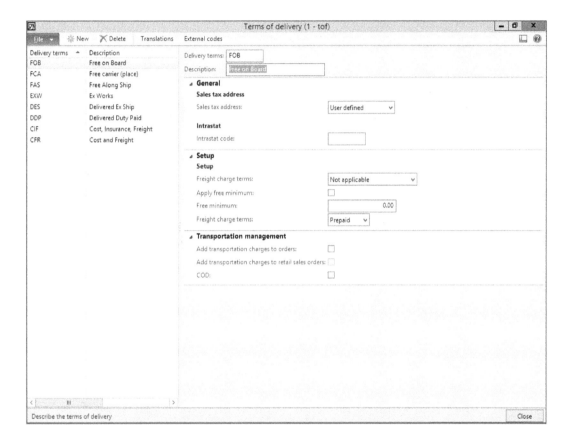

Click on the New button again to add the final record and then set the **Delivery Terms** code to **FOB** and the **Description** to **Free On Board**.

Configuring Modes Of Delivery

Next we will want to configure some default **Modes Of Delivery**.

Configuring Modes Of Delivery

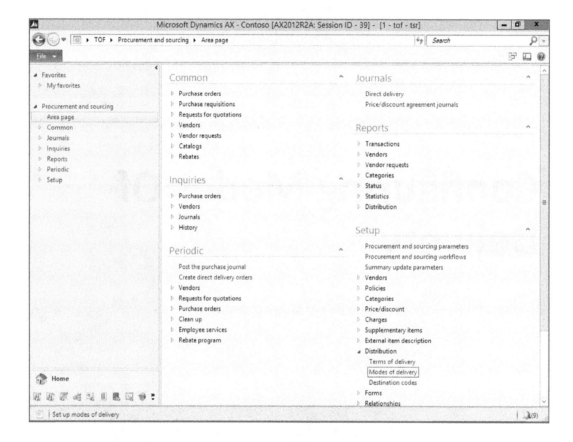

To do this, click on the **Modes of Delivery** menu item within the **Distribution** folder of the **Setup** group within the **Procurement and Sourcing** area page.

Configuring Modes Of Delivery

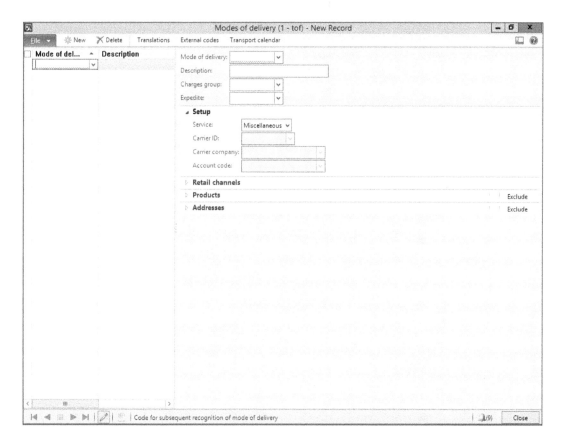

When the **Modes of Delivery** maintenance form is displayed, click on the **New** button in the menu bar to create a new record.

Configuring Modes Of Delivery

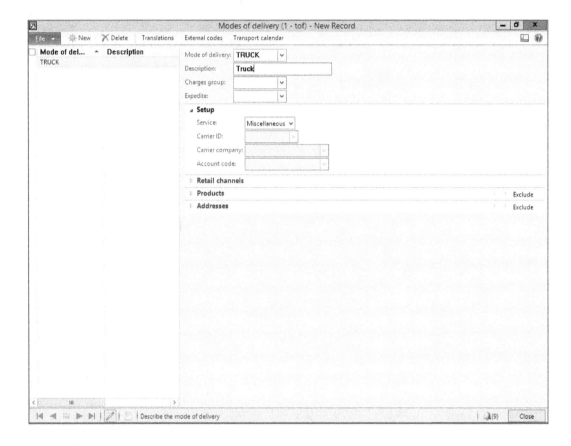

Set the **Mode of Delivery** code to **TRUCK** and the **Description** to **Truck.**

Configuring Modes Of Delivery

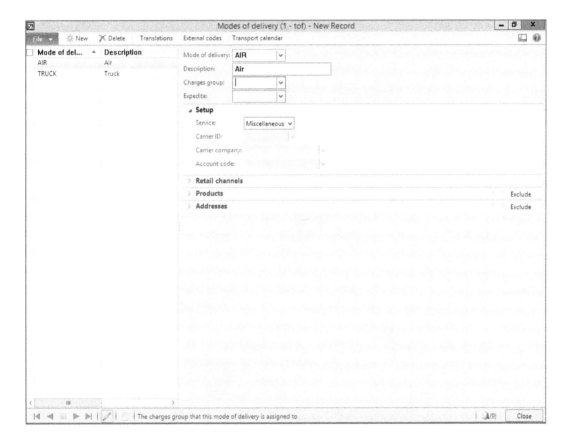

Click on the **New** button in the menu bar to create a new record and then set the **Mode of Delivery** code to **AIR** and the **Description** to **Air.**

Configuring Modes Of Delivery

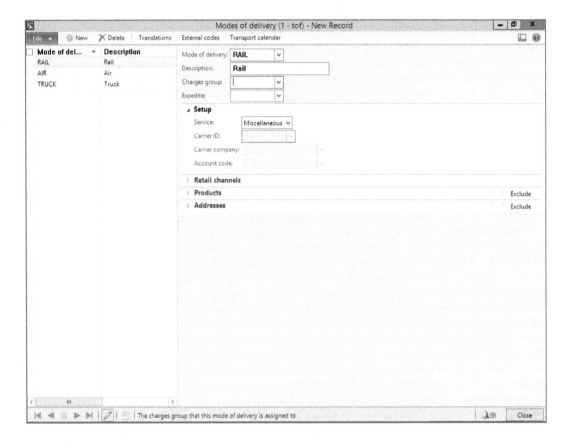

Click on the **New** button in the menu bar again to create a new record and then set the **Mode of Delivery** code to **RAIL** and the **Description** to **Rail.**

Configuring Modes Of Delivery

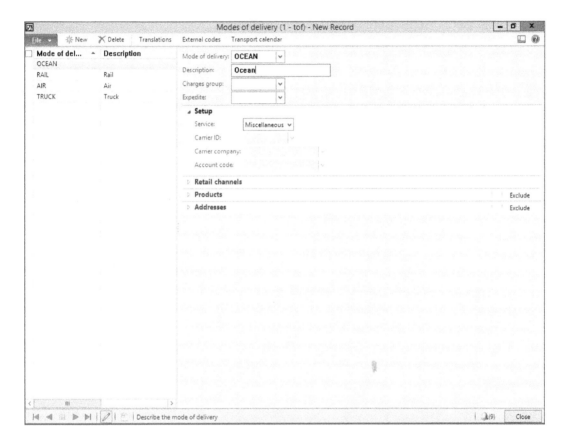

Click on the **New** button in the menu bar again to create a new record and then set the **Mode of Delivery** code to **OCEAN** and the **Description** to **Ocean.**

Configuring Modes Of Delivery

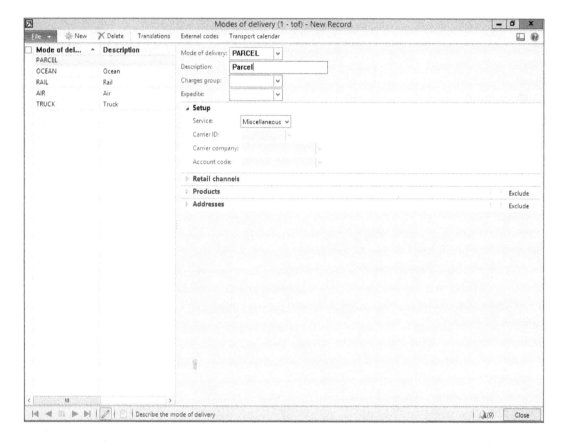

Click on the **New** button in the menu bar again to create a new record and then set the **Mode of Delivery** code to **PARCEL** and the **Description** to **Parcel.**

Configuring Modes Of Delivery

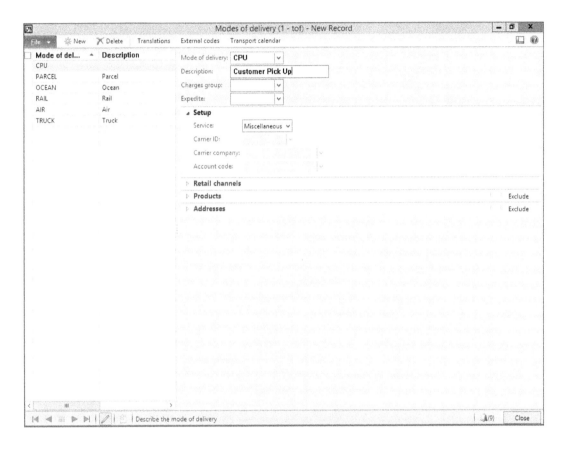

Click on the **New** button in the menu bar again to create the final record and then set the **Mode of Delivery** code to **CPU** and the **Description** to **Customer Pick Up.**

Configuring The Procurement and Sourcing Parameters

The is one last bit of setup that we need to perform, and that is just to tweak some of the **Procurement Parameters** to make sure that our purchase orders will run smoothly.

Configuring The Procurement and Sourcing Parameters

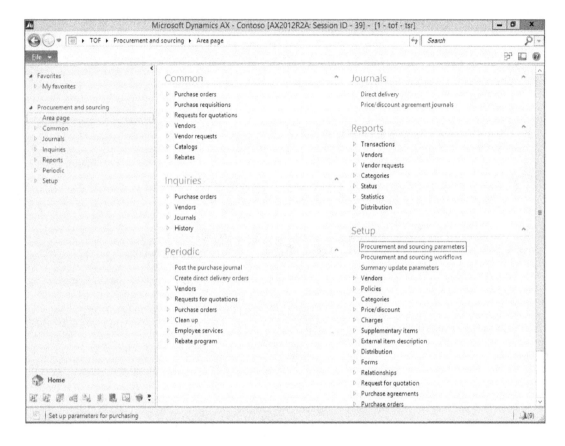

To do this, click on the **Procurement and Sourcing Parameters** menu item within the **Setup** group of the **Procurement and Sourcing** area page.

Configuring The Procurement and Sourcing Parameters

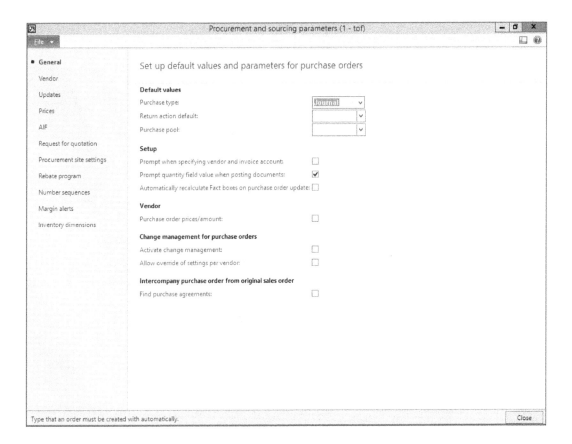

When the **Procurement and Sourcing Parameters** form is displayed, change to the **General** page (if it's not already selected).

Configuring The Procurement and Sourcing Parameters

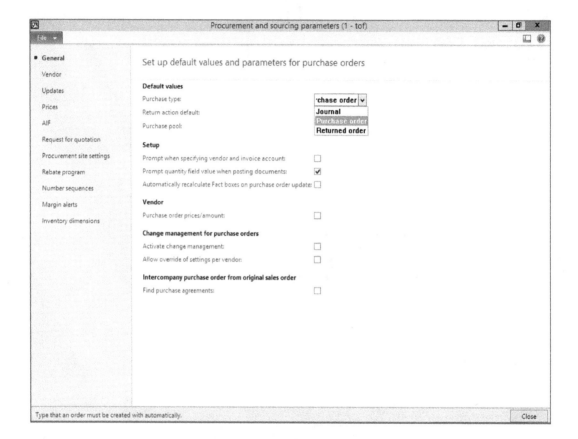

Click on the **Purchase Type** dropdown and select the **Purchase Order Type**

Note: By default the type is **Journal** which does not allow you to receive any product, so this is a very important change to make.

Configuring The Procurement and Sourcing Parameters

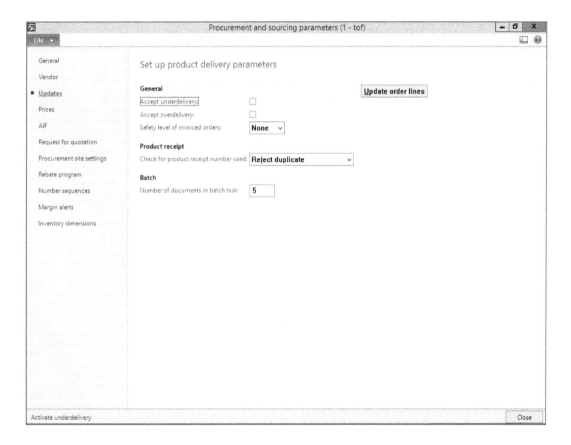

Then switch to the **Updates** page on the parameters form.

Configuring The Procurement and Sourcing Parameters

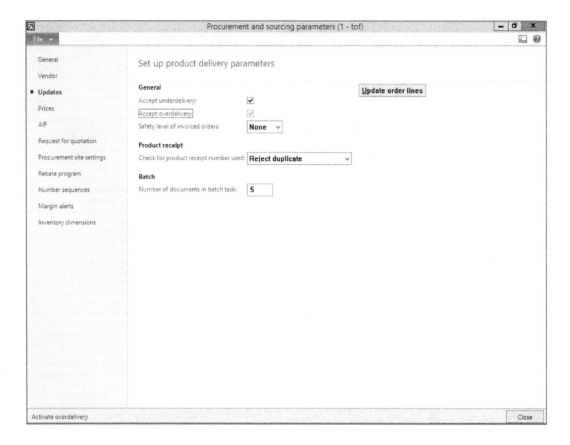

Check the **Accept Underdelivery** and **Accept Overdelivery** flags so that you can accept shipments that are not exactly the quantity that you asked for.

Configuring The Procurement and Sourcing Parameters

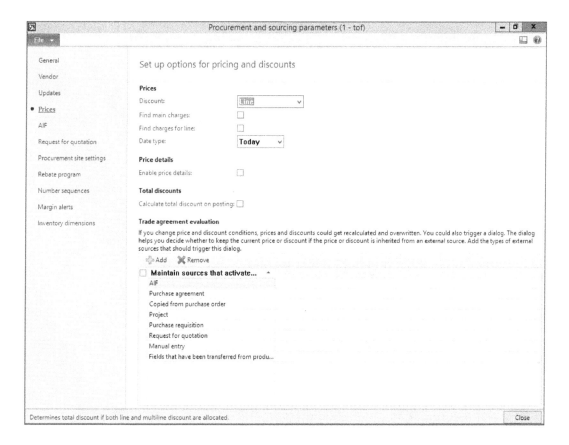

Then switch to the **Prices** page on the parameters form.

Configuring The Procurement and Sourcing Parameters

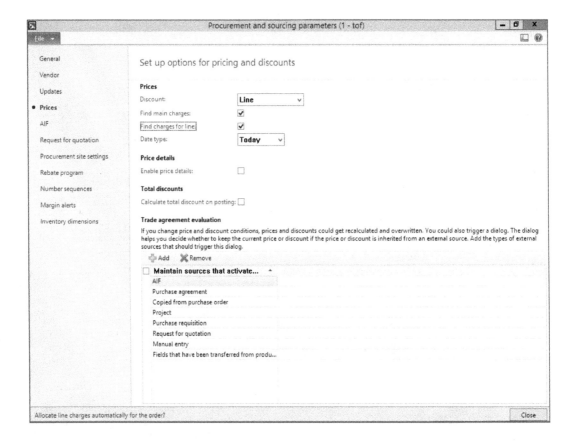

On this page, check the **Find Main Charges** flag and also the **Find Charges for Lines** flag just in case you want to use the additional charges capability within purchasing.

Configuring The Procurement and Sourcing Parameters

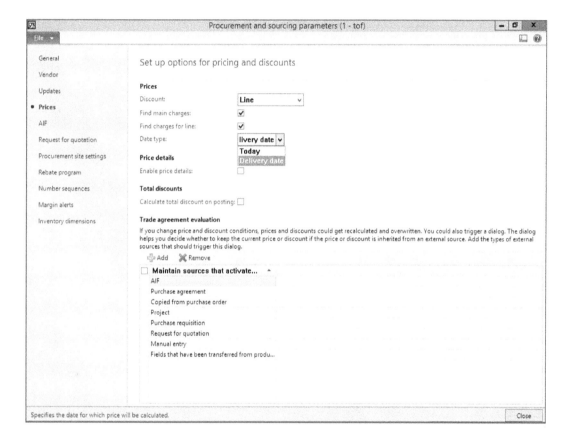

Then click on the **Date Type** dropdown and select the **Delivery Date**, which will allow the system calculate the purchase prices based on the delivery date and not the ordered date.

Configuring The Procurement and Sourcing Parameters

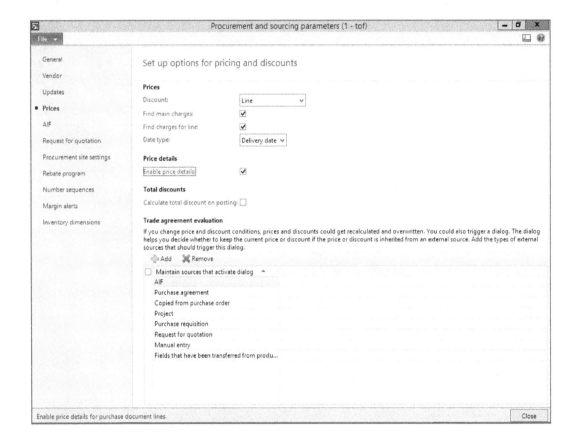

Also check the **Enable Price Details** flag which will allow us to see how Purchase Prices are calculated on the Purchase Orders later on.

Configuring The Procurement and Sourcing Parameters

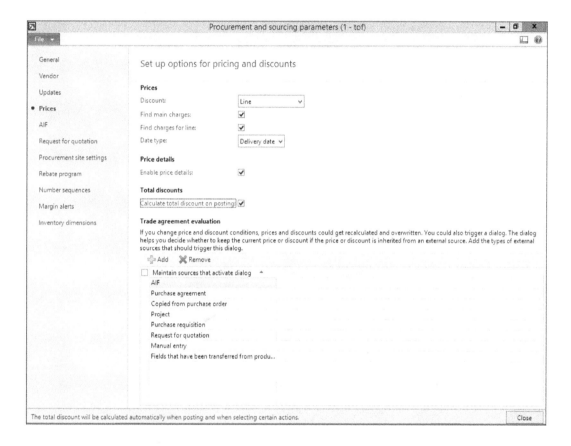

Also check the **Calculate Total Discount On Posting** checkbox.

After you have done that then you are all done, and you can click on the **Close** button to exit from the form.

CONFIGURING PROCUREMENT CATEGORIES

Sometimes spending a little bit of time in advance can save you a lot of time in the long run. One example of this is that if you set up the **Procurement Categories** within Procurement and Sourcing, you will be able to use them later on in setup time. So in this chapter we will show you how you can set them up and link them with you Products and Vendors.

Configuring Procurement Hierarchies

The **Procurement Categories** are all based of a category hierarchy that you set up within Dynamics AX. So the first step is to build a **Category Hierarchy** that you will then link to the Procurement & Sourcing module.

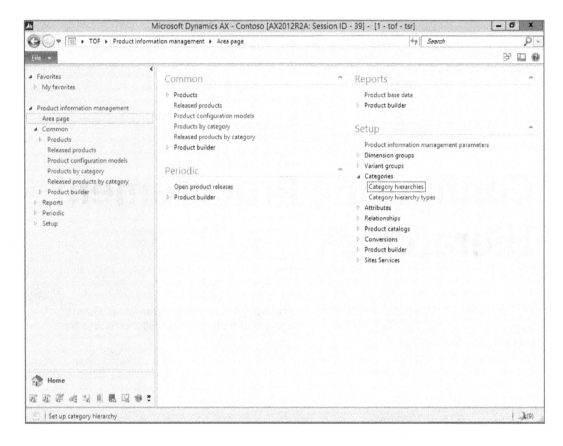

To do this, click on the **Category Hierarchies** menu item within the **Categories** folder of the
Setup group within the **Product Information Management** area page.

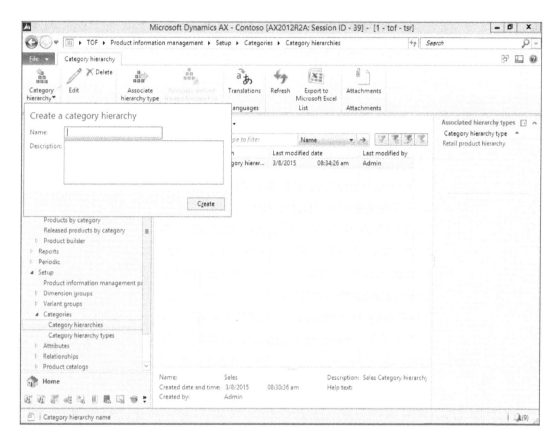

When the **Category Hierarchies** list page is displayed, click on the **Category Hierarchy** button within the **New** group of the **Category Hierarchy** ribbon bar.

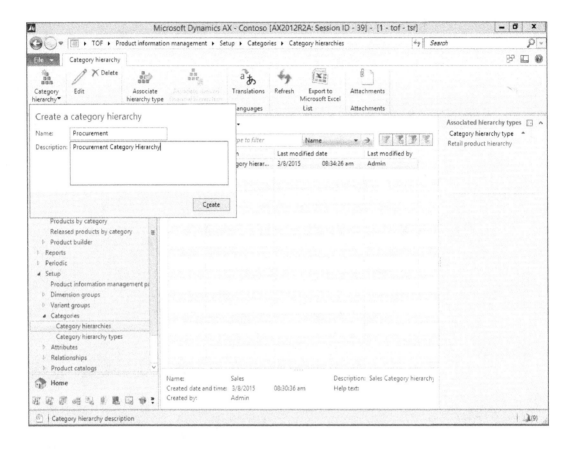

When the **Create a Category Hierarchy** dialog box is displayed set the **Name** to **Procurement** and the **Description** to **Procurement Category Hierarchy**.

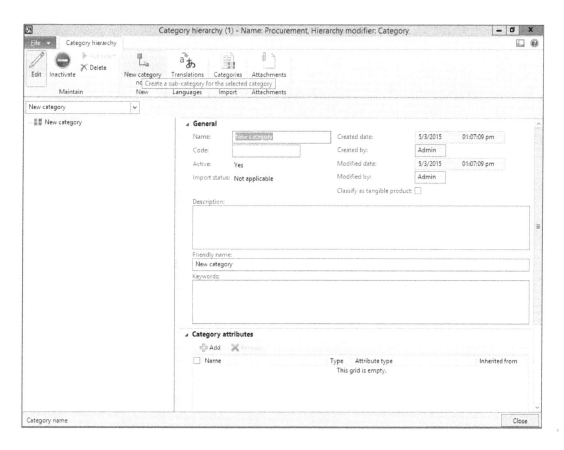

When the **Category Hierarchy** maintenance form is displayed, click on the **New Category Node** button within the **New** group of the **Category Hierarchy** ribbon bar.

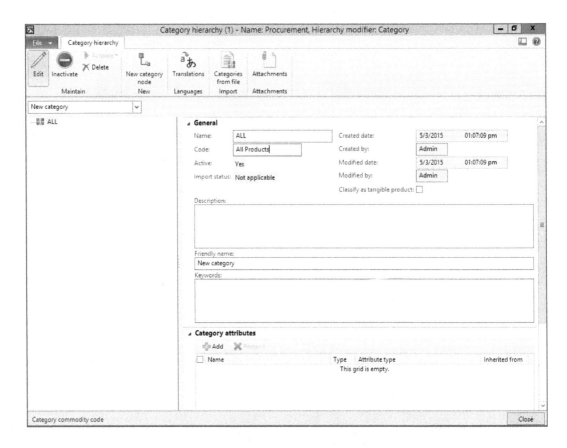

For the top level of the hierarchy, set the **Name** to **ALL** and the **Code** to **All Products**.

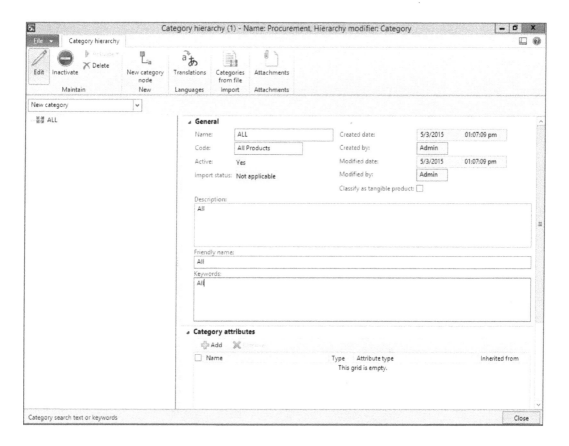

Then set the **Description**, **Friendly Name**, and **Keywords** to **All** as well.

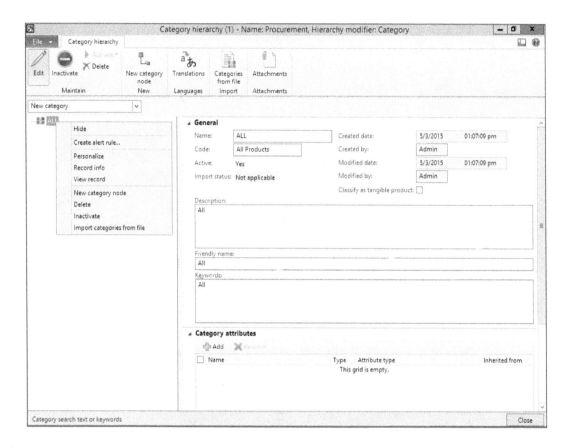

Now we want to create some child categories below the parent. To do this, right-mouse-click on the **ALL** node and select the **New Category Node** menu item within the pop-up menu.

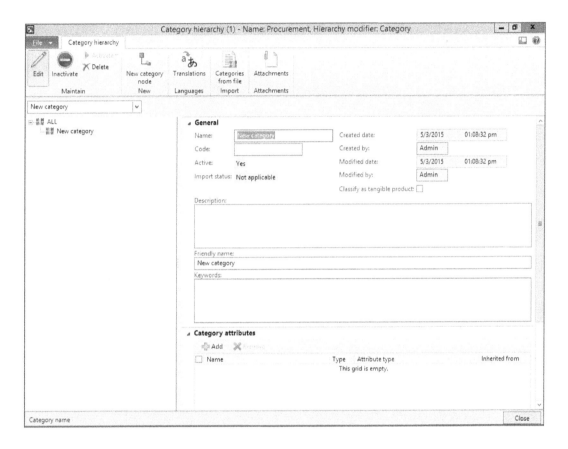

This will create a new child node.

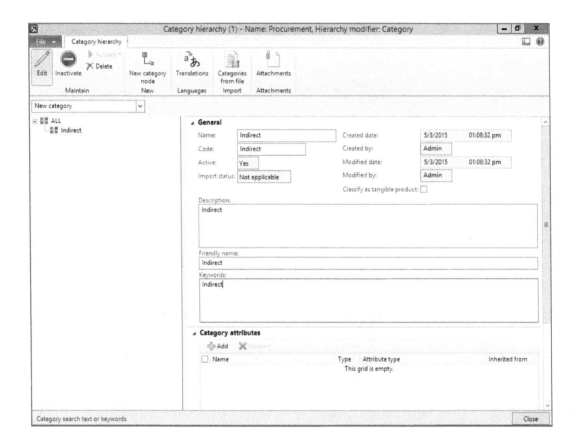

Set the **Name, Code, Description, Friendly Name** and **Keywords** to **Indirect**.

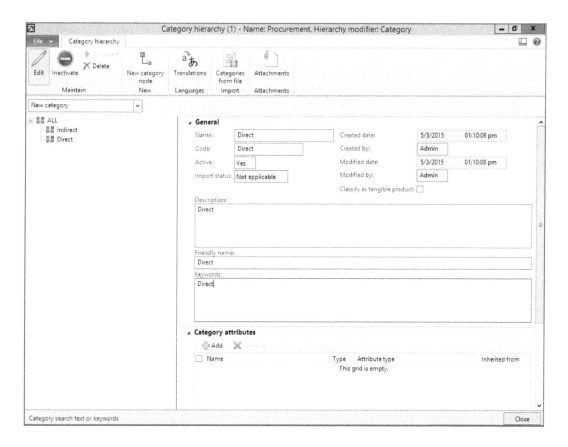

Repeat the process again to create another category below the ALL category and set the **Name**, **Code**, **Description**, **Friendly Name** and **Keywords** to **Direct.**

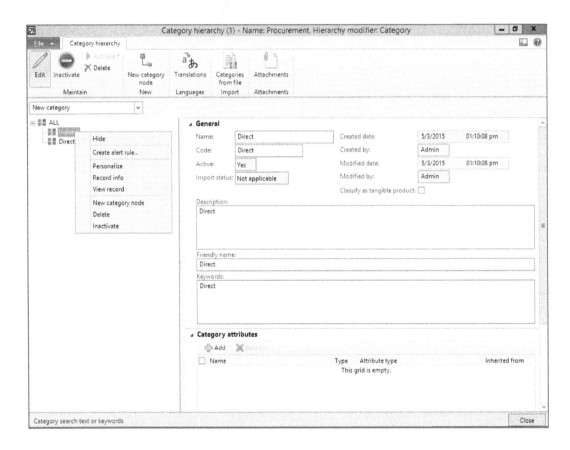

Now we will create some categories below the main categories that we just created. So right-mouse-click on the **Indirect** category and select the **New Category Node** sub-menu item.

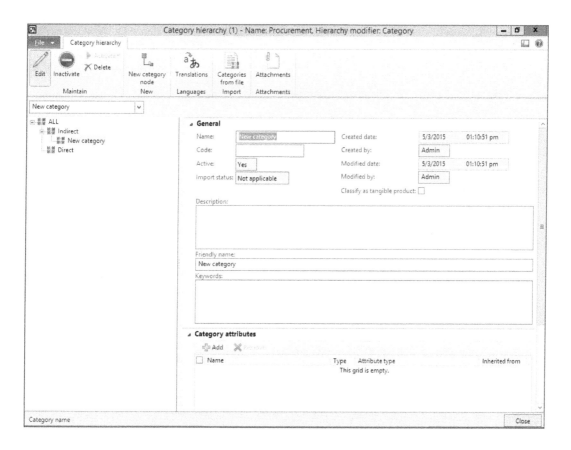

Now you will have a category below the **Indirect** category.

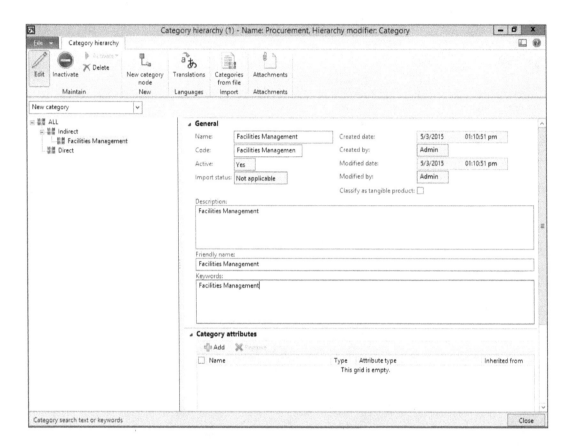

Set the **Name**, **Code**, **Description**, **Friendly Name** and **Keywords** to **Facilities Management**.

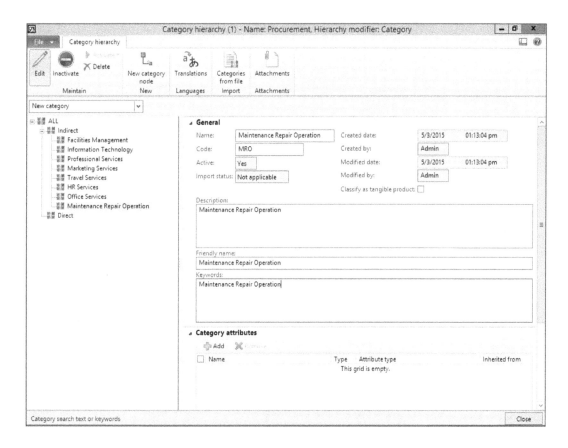

Repeat the process a couple more times and add the following Categories:

Information Technology
Professional Services
Marketing Services
Travel Services
HR Services
Office Supplies
Maintenance Repair Operations

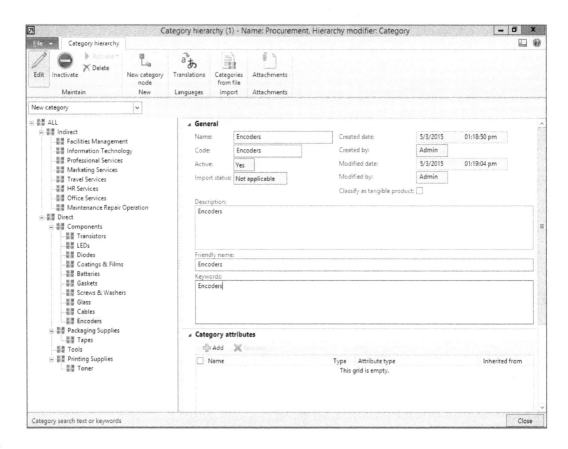

Now add the following Sub-Nodes to the **Direct** category:

Components   Packaging Supplies
 Transistors   Tapes
 LEDs   Tools
 Diodes   Printing Supplies
 Coating & Films   Toner
 Batteries
 Gaskets
 Screws & Washers
 Glass
 Cables
 Encoders

After you are done, click on the **Close** button to exit from the form.

Configuring Category Hierarchy Types

Next we want to link the **Category Hierarchy** that we just created to the **Procurement & Sourcing** module so that we can use it to set up the purchasing details.

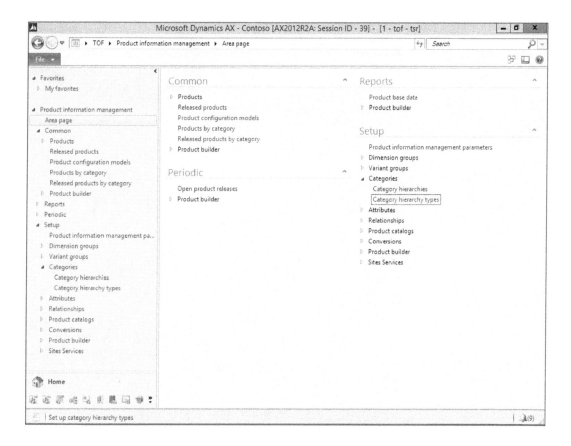

To do this, click on the **Category Hierarchy Types** menu item within the **Categories** folder of the **Setup** group within the **Product Information Management** area page.

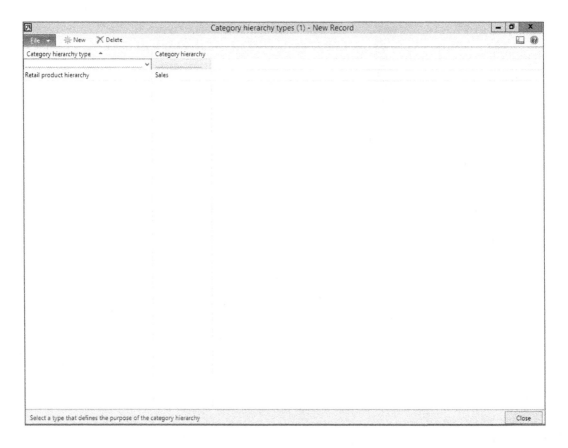

When the **Category Hierarchy Types** maintenance form is displayed, click on the **New** button to create a new record

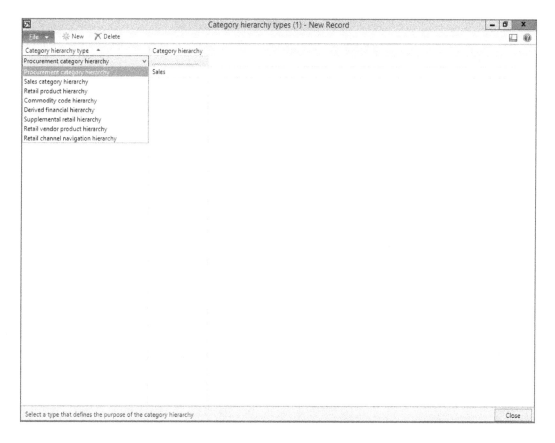

Click on the **Category Hierarchy Type** dropdown and select the **Procurement Category Hierarchy** option.

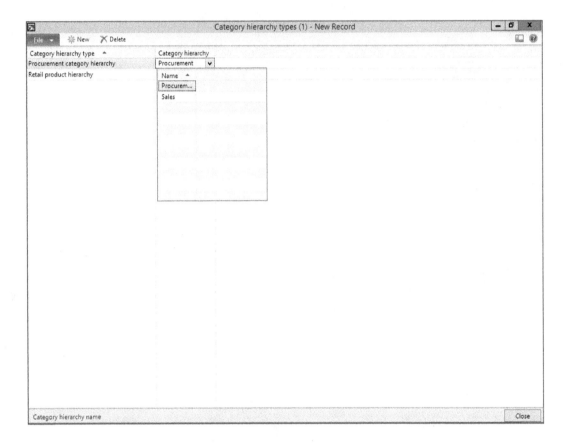

Then click on the **Category Hierarchy** dropdown list and select the **Procurement** category that you just created.

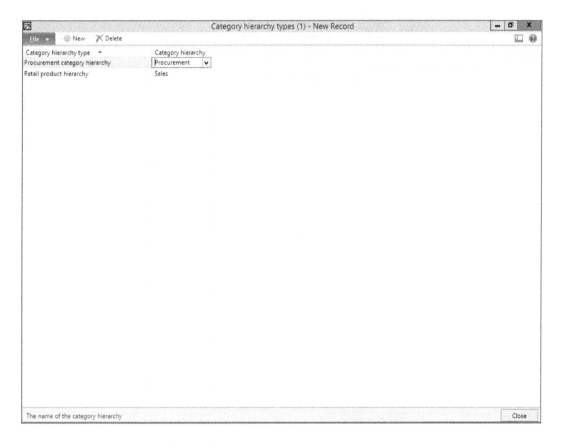

After you have done that click on the **Close** button to exit from the form.

Assigning Products To Procurement Categories

Now that we have built our **Procurement Categories**, we can start assigning our products to them for the procurement processes.

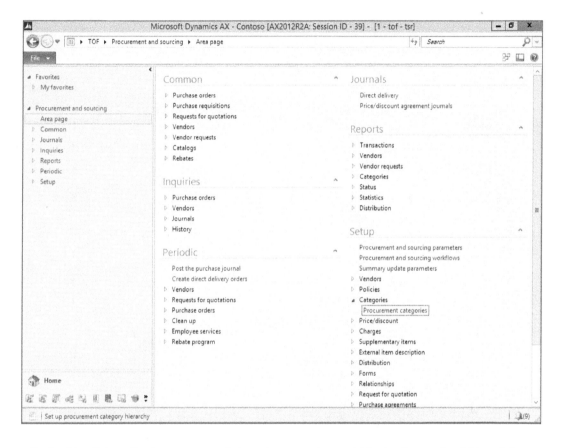

To do this, click on the **Procurement Categories** menu item within the **Categories** folder of the **Setup** group within the **Procurement and Sourcing** area page.

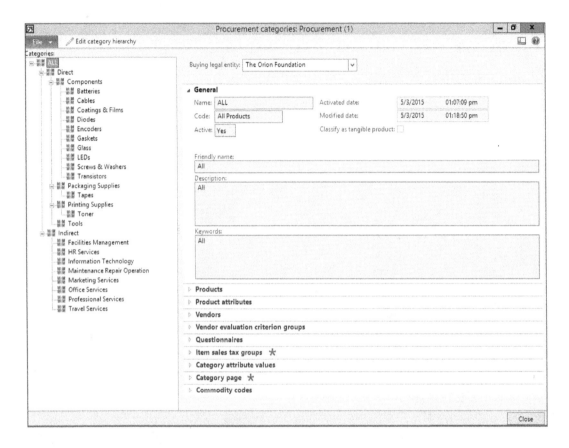

When the **Procurement Categories** maintenance form is displayed, you will see that all of the categories that you set up within the **Category Hierarchy** will be waiting for you.

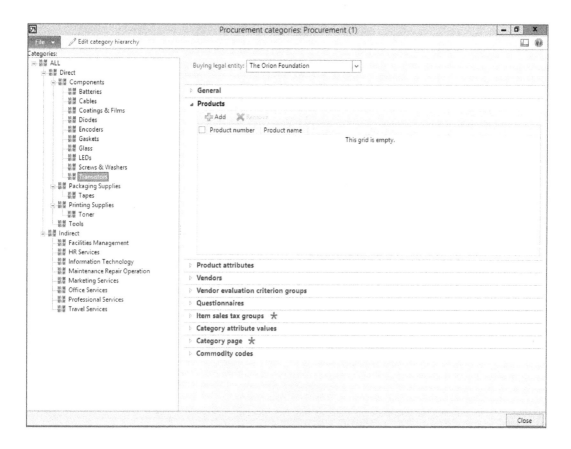

To add products to the category, select the **Category** that you want to populate (Transistors seems like as good of a place to start as any), expand out the **Products** tab group within the details pane, and then click on the **Add** button within the tabs menu bar.

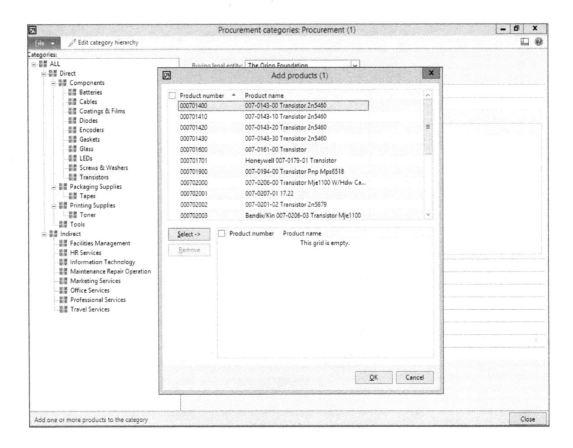

This will open up a list of all the products that you have loaded into the system.

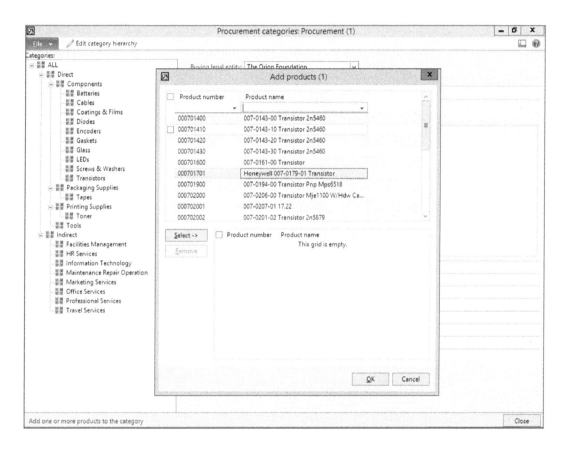

You can add the products individually be selecting the product and then clicking on the **Select** button, but there is an easier way. Start off by pressing **CTRL+G** to open up the filter by grid line in the table form.

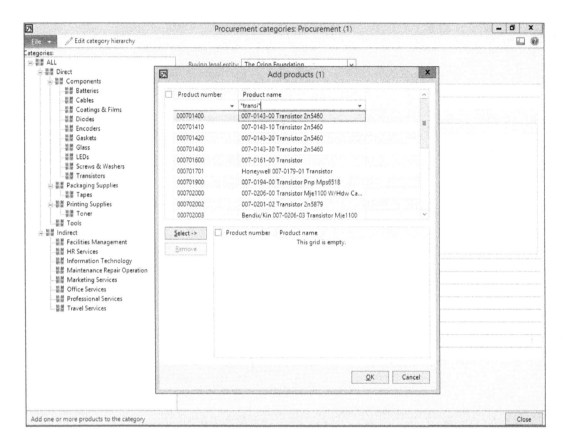

Now type in a wildcard to filter out your products. In this case we just used ***transi*** to find all of the transistors.

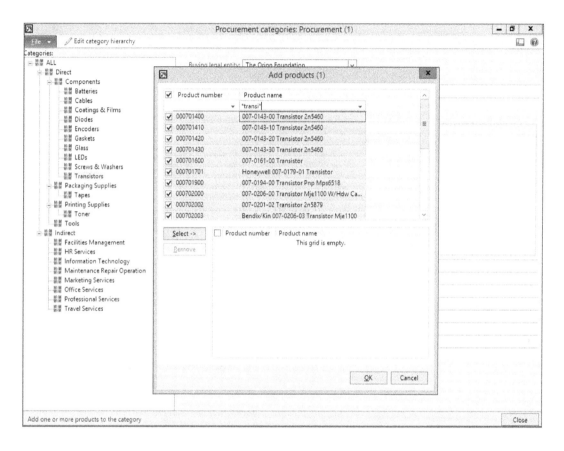

Now click on the **Select All** checkbox in the top right of the form to select all of the products.

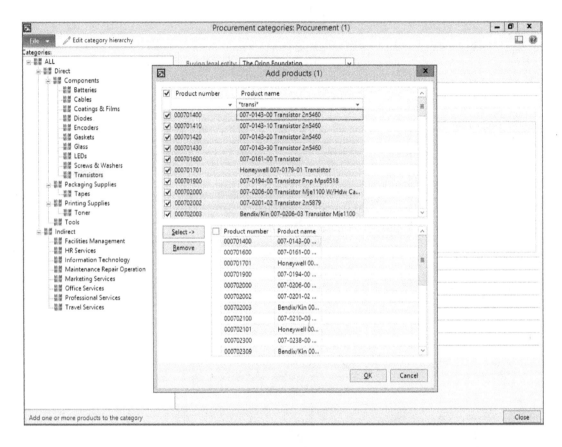

Then click on the **Select** button to add them to the selection list. Then click on the **OK** button.

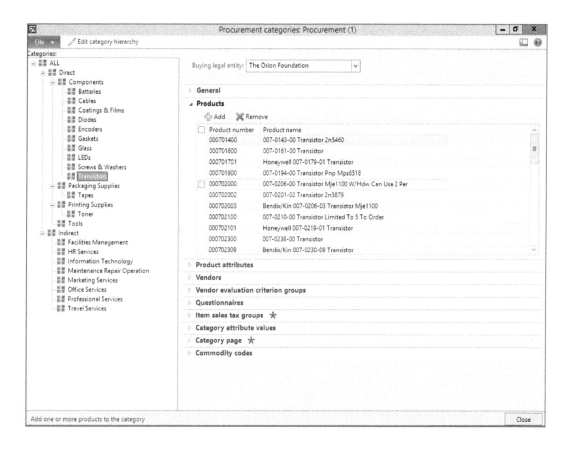

Now all of the products will show up within the **Products** tab group of the **Procurement Categories**.

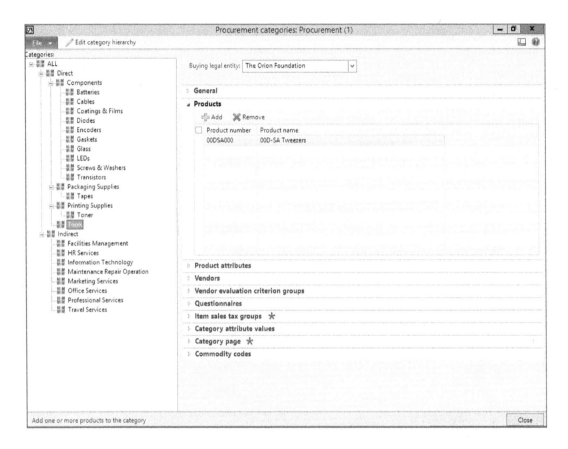

Repeat the process for all of the other **Procurement Categories** and when you are done, just click on the **Close** button to exit from the form.

Assigning Vendors To Procurement Categories

You can also assign your default vendors to the Product Categories so that you can identify the preferred vendors by category.

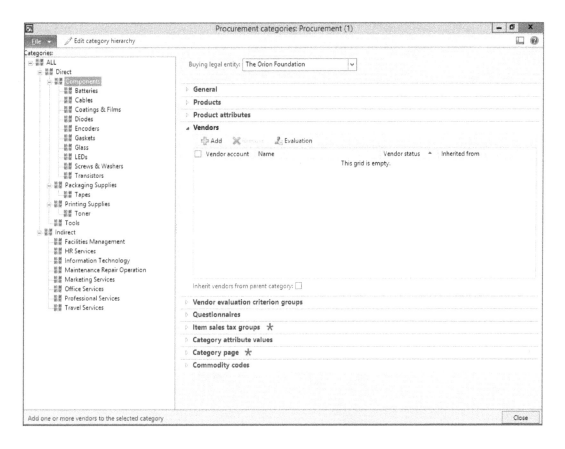

To do this select a **Procurement Category** (we will select the **Components** category for this one) expand out the **Vendors** tab group within the details pane and then click on the **Add** button.

Note: In this case we ware not selecting the leaf nodes, because we want to assign the vendors to all of the child categories.

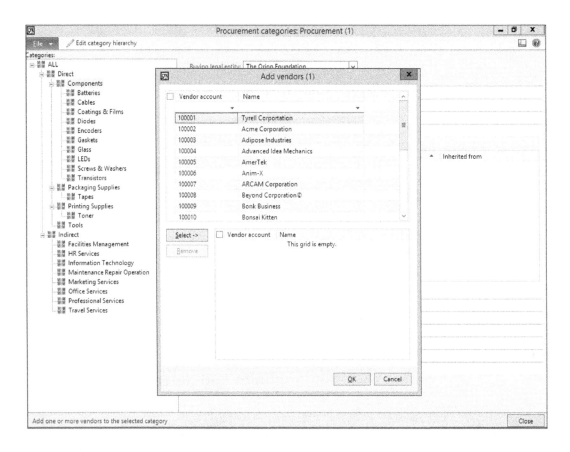

This will open up the **Add Vendors** dialog box.

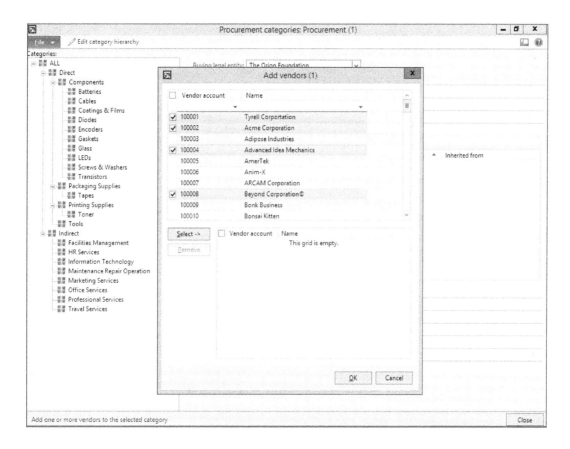

All you need to do is select all of the vendors that you want to assign to the category.

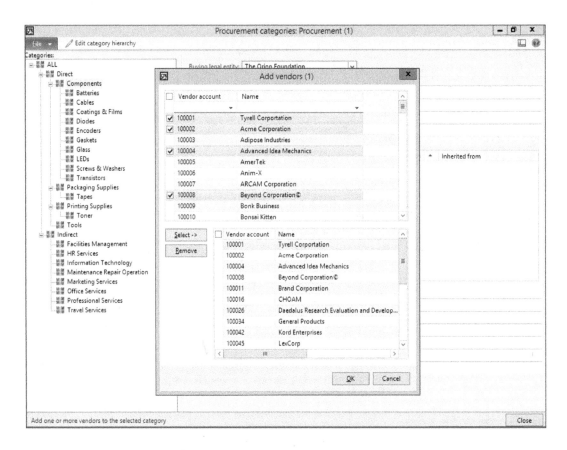

And then click on the **Select** button to add hem to the selected list. When you are done, click
on the **OK** button to exit from the form.

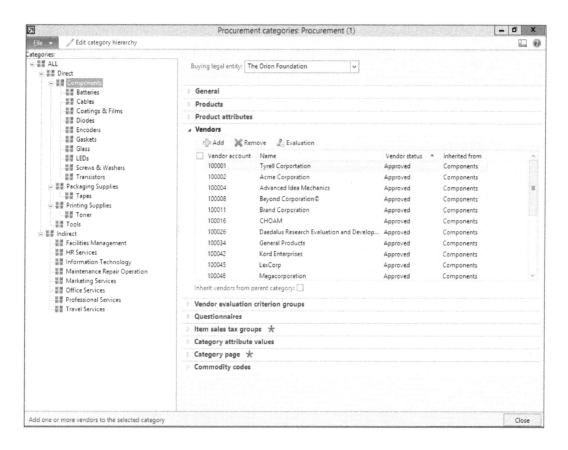

When you return back to the **Procurement Categories** form you will see that the vendors have been added to the category.

You can keep on updating all of the other categories if you like.

Inheriting Approved Vendors From Parent Categories

There is a nifty feature within the Categories maintenance form for both the products and vendors which allows child categories to inherit values form their parent categories. This can save a lot of rekeying if you take advantage of it.

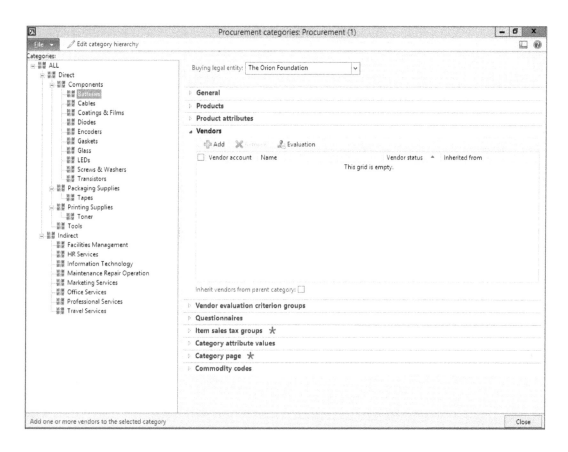

To do this, just open up the child category that you want to inherit the parent settings from. Then also open up the data panel that you want to inherit – in this case we are choosing the **Vendors**.

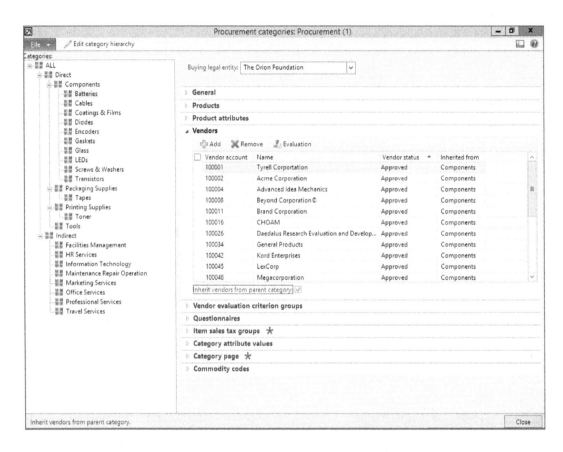

All you need to do is check the **Inherit Vendors from Parent Category** flag and the parents vendors will automatically populate from the parent. You can update all of the other categories if you like and when you are done, just click on the **Close** button to exit from the form.

PROCESSING PURCHASE ORDERS

Now that we have all of the codes and controls set up we can start creating **Purchase Orders**, receive them and then post them as Payables Invoices.

In this chapter we will step you though that process.

Creating a Purchase Order

The first step is to create a Purchase Order.

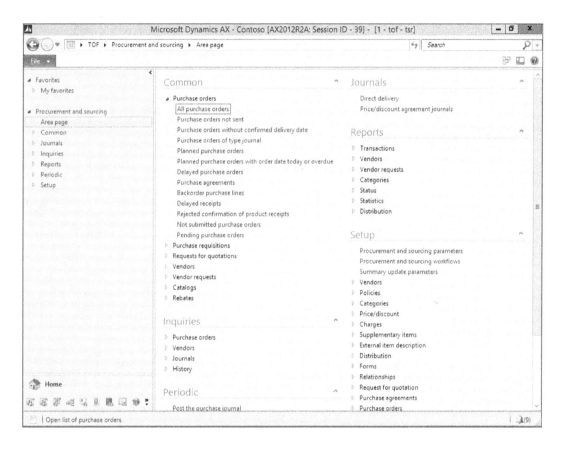

To do this click on the **All Purchase Orders** menu item within the **Purchase Orders** folder of the **Common** group within the **Procurement and Sourcing** area page.

When the **All Purchase Orders** list page is displayed, click on the **Purchase Order** button within the **New** group of the **Purchase Order** ribbon mar to create a new Purchase Order.

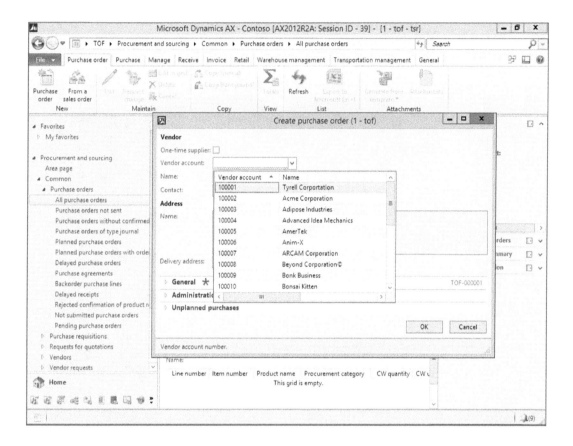

When the **Create New Purchase Order** quick creation dialog is displayed, click on the **Vendor Account** dropdown list to see the list of all of your vendors, and select the vendor that you want to create the Purchase Order for.

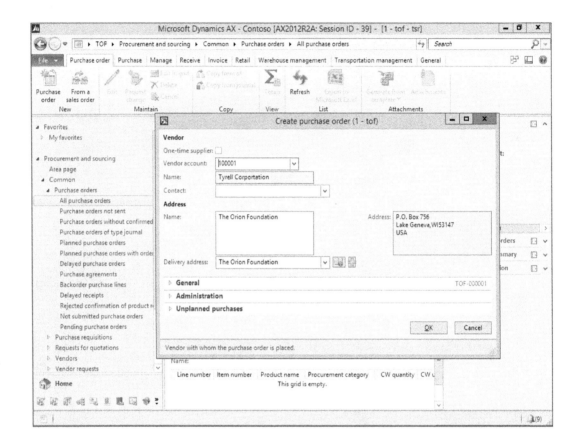

This will populate all of the address details.

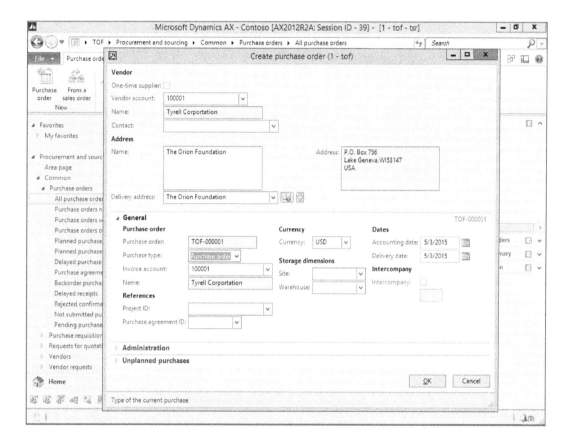

If you expand out the **General** tab group then you will also see that there are more details that you can set up for your Purchase Order.

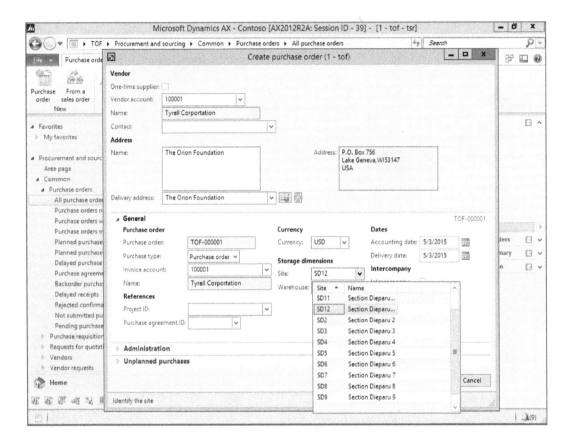

To make things a little easier, you can set up the default **Site** and **Warehouse** so that you don't they will default into the Purchase Order Lines. To do this, click on the **Site** dropdown list and select the default site – in this example we will use **SD12**.

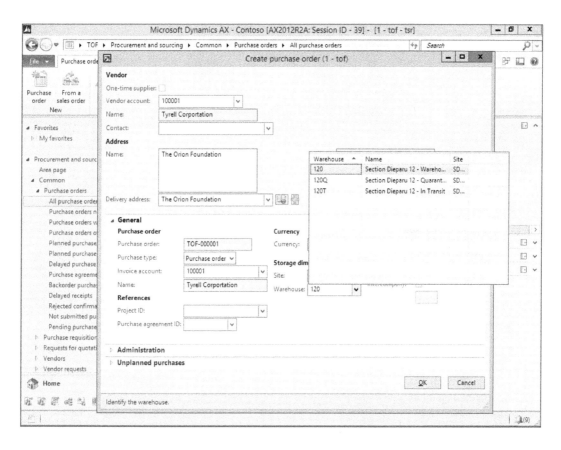

Then click on the **Warehouse** dropdown list and select the **Warehouse** that you want to receive the Purchase Order into. In this example we will choose **120**.

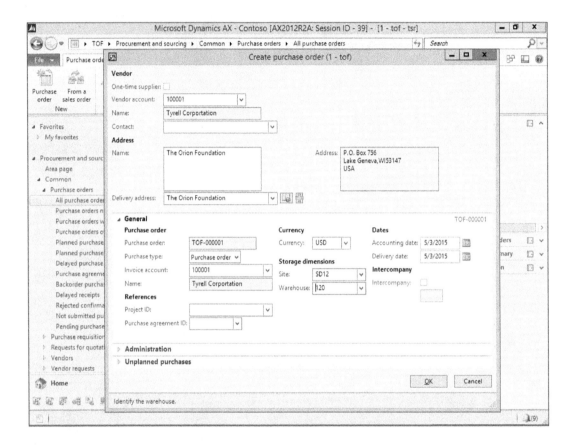

When you are done, just click on the **OK** button to create the Purchase Order.

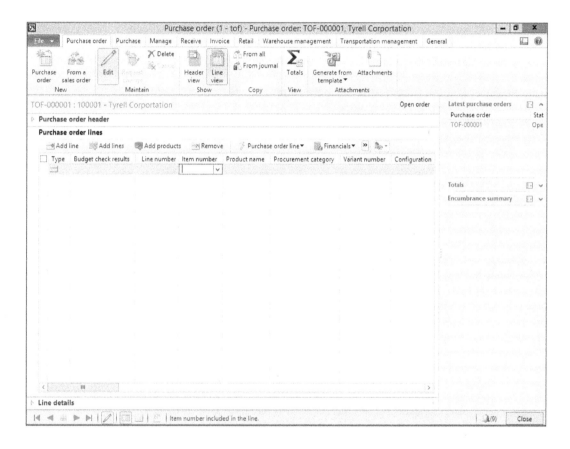

This will open up the **Purchase Order** detail form where you can start entering in the Purchase Order Lines.

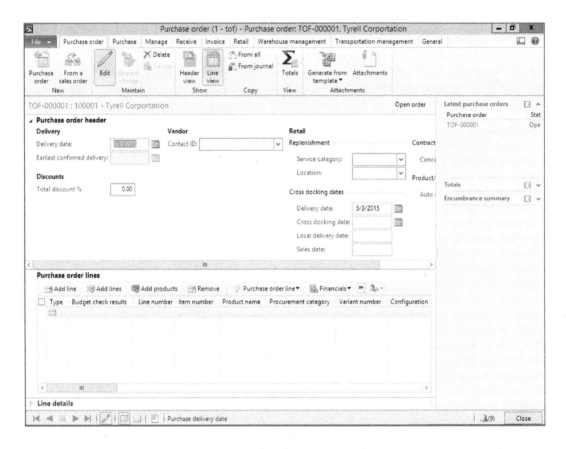

If you expand the **Purchase Order Header** tab then you will see some of the header information
for the purchase order. You can quickly update some of the default information from the
header here if you like, and then just compact the tab by clicking on the **Purchase Order
Header** header again.

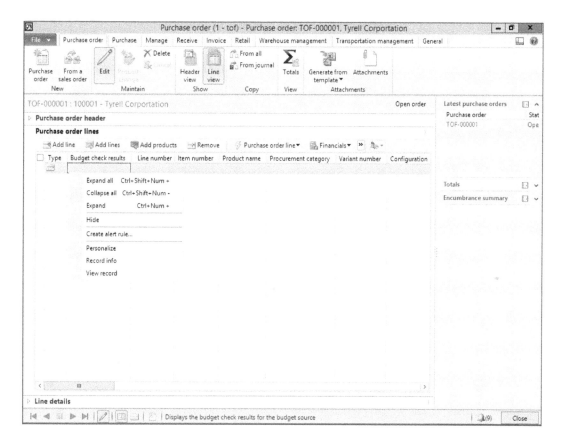

Since this is the first time that we are going into the **Purchase Order Details** form there are a few fields that we don't need to see right now, so we will tidy it up by hiding some of them. Start off by right-mouse-clicking on the **Budget Results** field and selecting the **Hide** sub-menu item.

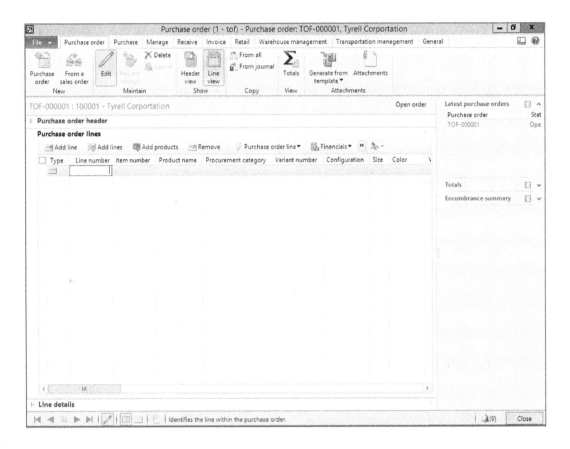

This will hide the field for you (not delete it).

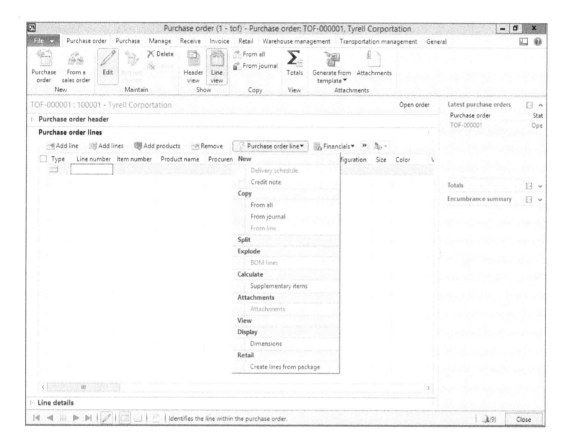

Also, there are a few inventory dimensions that we don't see – like the **Site** and **Warehouse**. You can turn them on through the **Dimensions** display. To do this, click on the **Purchase Order Lines** menu within the **Purchase Order Lines** tab and select the **Dimensions** submenu item.

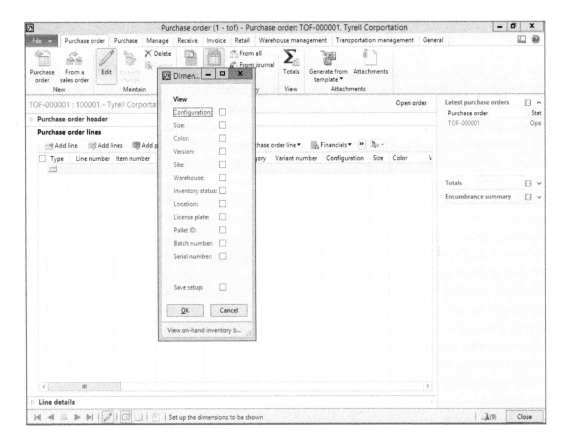

This will open up the **Dimension** browser where you can see all of the different dimensions that you can show on the **Purchase Order Line**.

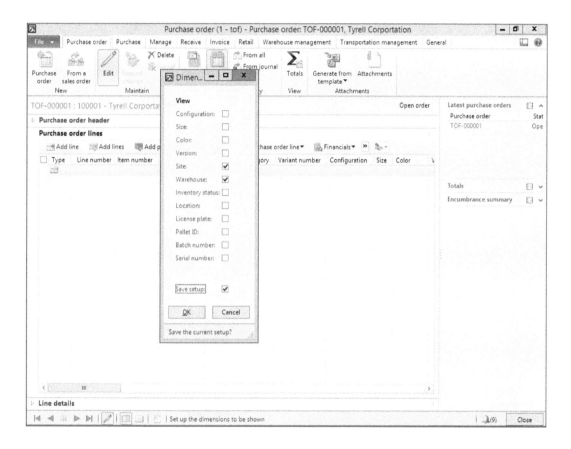

Check the **Site** and **Warehouse** dimensions and then click on the **Save Setup** flag to tell the system that you always want to show them. If you don't do this then you will just see the dimensions for this instance of the form, and then it will revert back to the default state. After you have done that click on the **OK** button to return back to the **Purchase Order Lines** form.

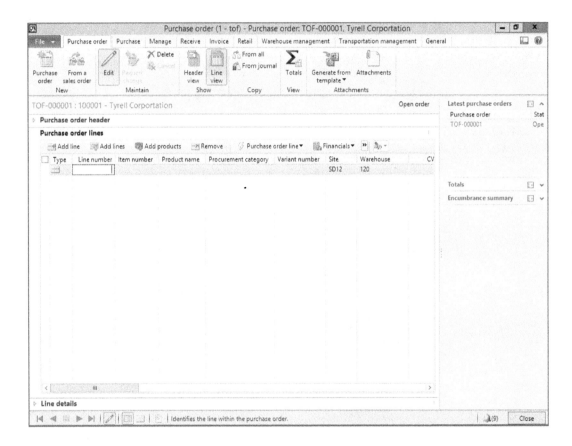

Now you will see that the **Site** and **Warehouse** are displayed of the form, and also defaulting in from the header defaults that you defined earlier on.

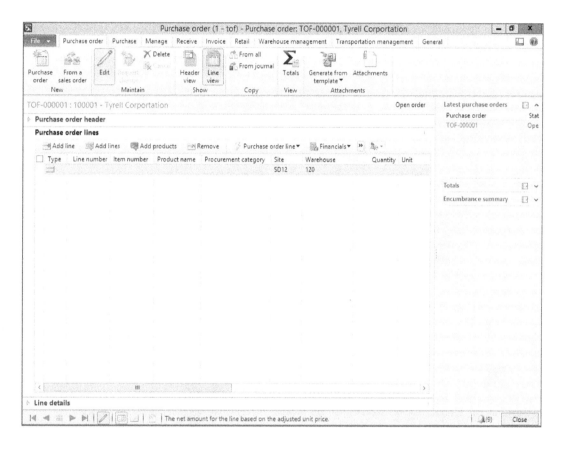

You can further tidy up the fields that are shown by hiding the fields that you don't need right now until you have all of the fields that you need showing up on the form. The key ones are the **Item Number**, **Quantity** and **Unit**.

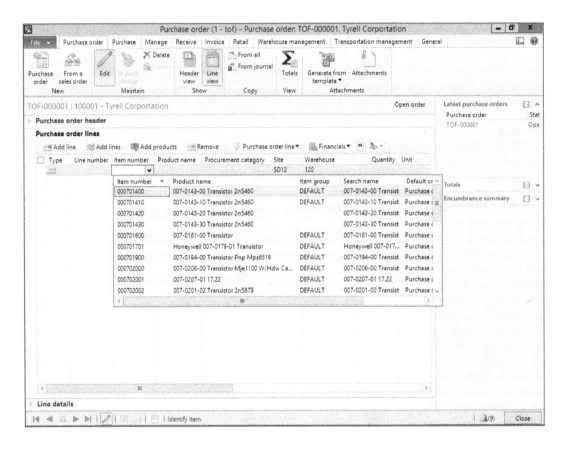

To add a line the old-school way just click on the **Item Number** dropdown list and select the item that you want to purchase,

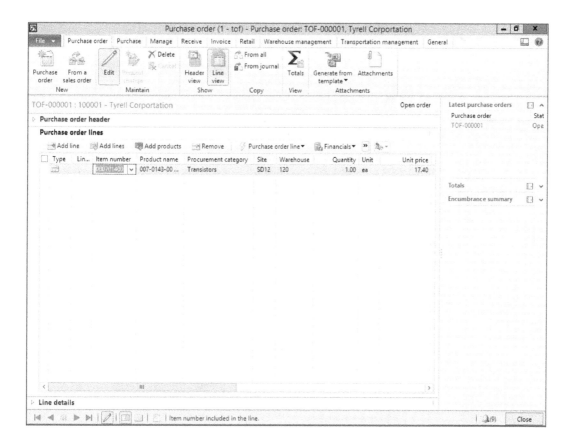

Just by doing this, the **Product Name**, **Procurement Category, Unit** and the **Price** will default in from the master tables.

Another way that you can add lines though is by clicking on the **Add Products** button on the **Purchase Order Lines** menu bar.

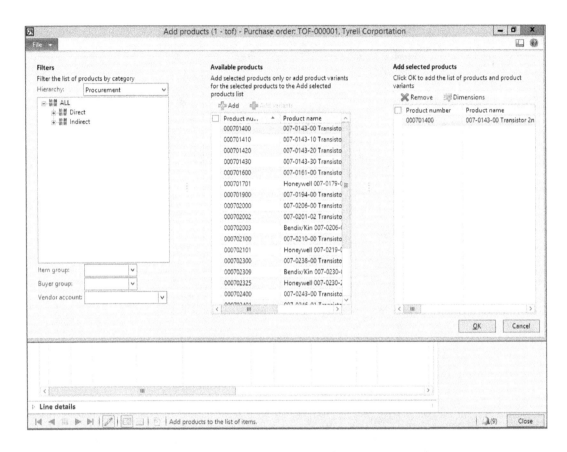

This will open up the **Add Products** selection form which shows all of your **Procurement Categories** that you set up and also all of the products that match.

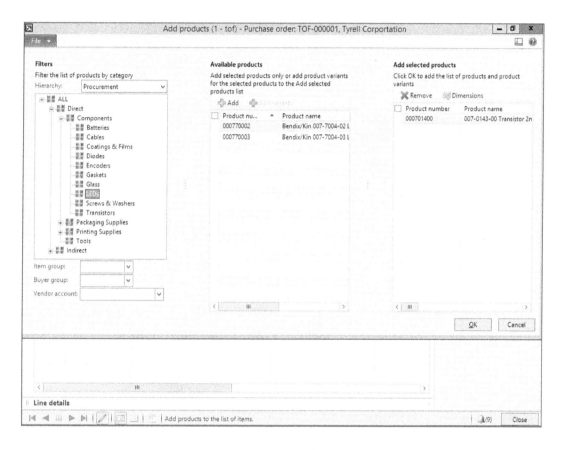

If you drill into the **Procurement Categories** then the list of products that are available will be filtered to match just those categories.

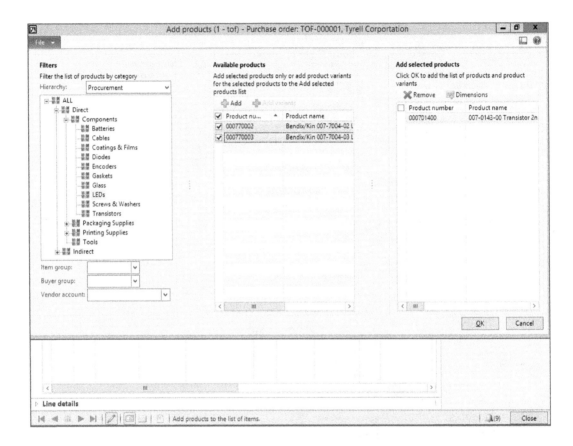

You can select one or more of the products and then click on the **Add** button within the **Available Products** column.

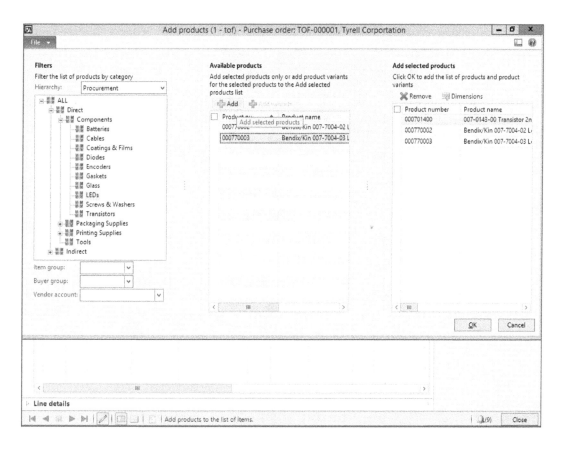

That will add them to the **Add Selected Products** column. When you have added all of the products that you need, just click on the **OK** button to add them to the **Purchase Order**.

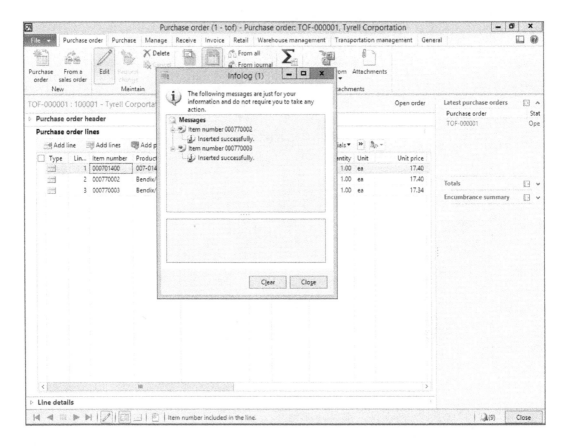

You will probably get a dialog box saying that the products have been added and you can just click on the **Close** button to dismiss the notice.

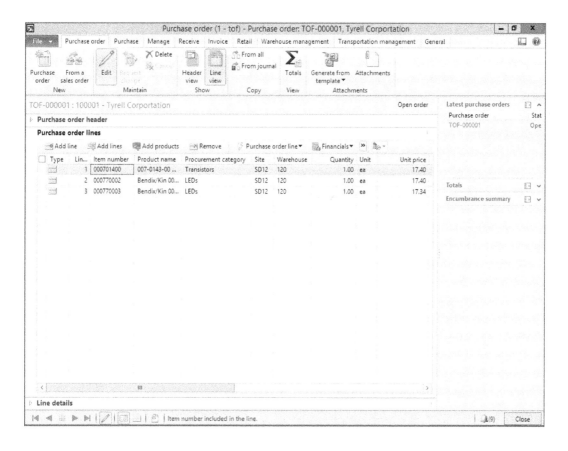

When you return to the **Purchase Order** you will see that the lines have been added for you.

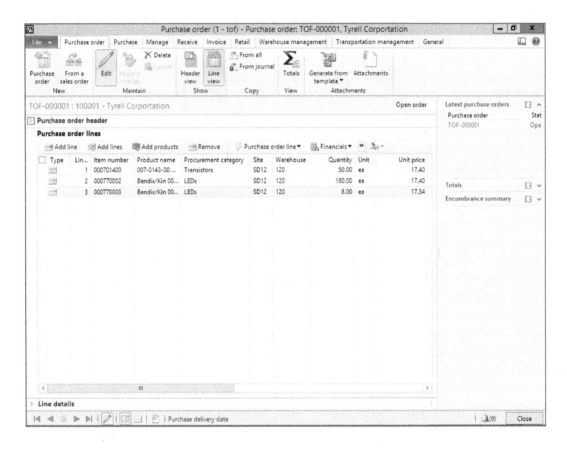

You can then update the **Quantities** for the lines.

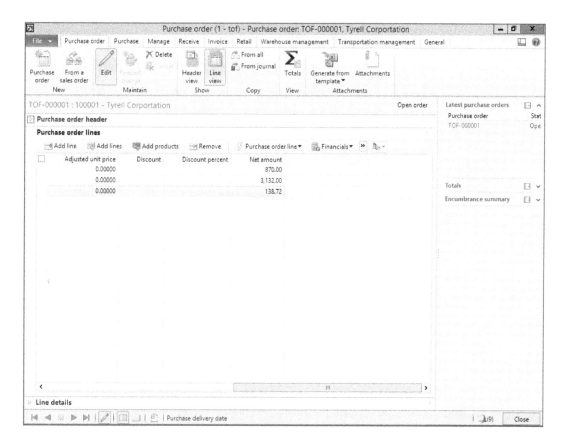

If you scroll over to the right a little on the **Purchase Order Lines** then you will also see that the **Net Amount** for the lines are being updated.

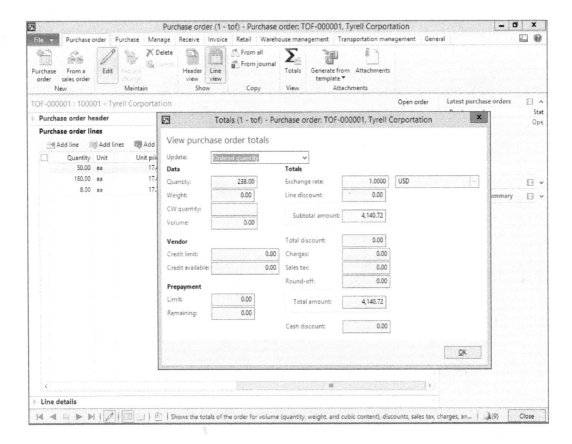

Also, if you click on the **Totals** button within the **View** group of the **Purchase Order** ribbon bar then you will be able to see a summary of the Purchase Order totals, including any discounts, tax, and additional charges that may have been applied.

You can click on the **OK** button to dismiss the form.

Confirming A Purchase Order

After you have created your purchase order, you can make it live by **Confirming** it. This does a number of things, including making it available for receipt, printing out the **Purchase Order Confirmation**, and even e-mailing the **Purchase Order** to the **Vendor** if you have the Print Management configured.

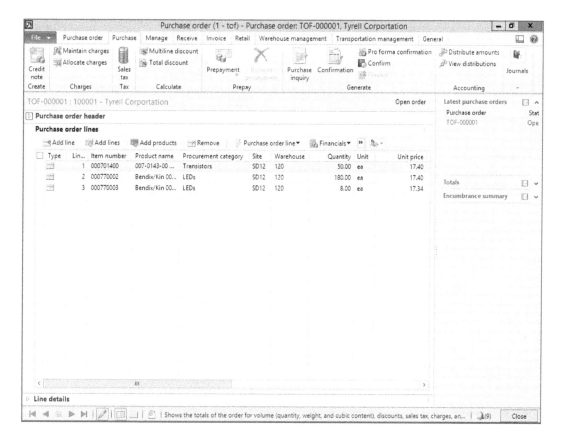

To confirm the **Purchase Order** just click on the **Confirmation** button within the **Generate** group of the **Purchase** ribbon bar.

This will open up the **Confirm Purchase Order** dialog box.

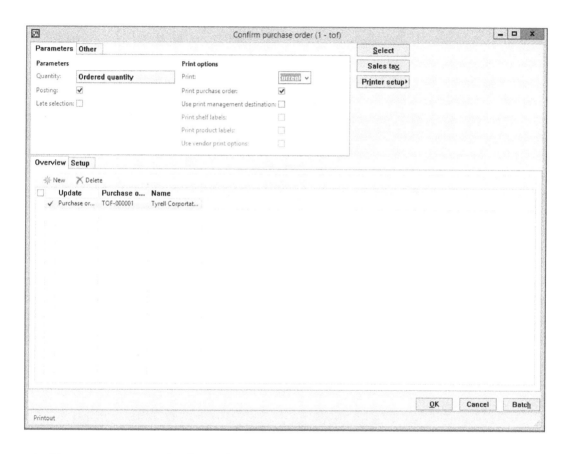

In this case we want to print the confirmation as well, so check the **Print Purchase Order** flag.

Then click on the **OK** button.

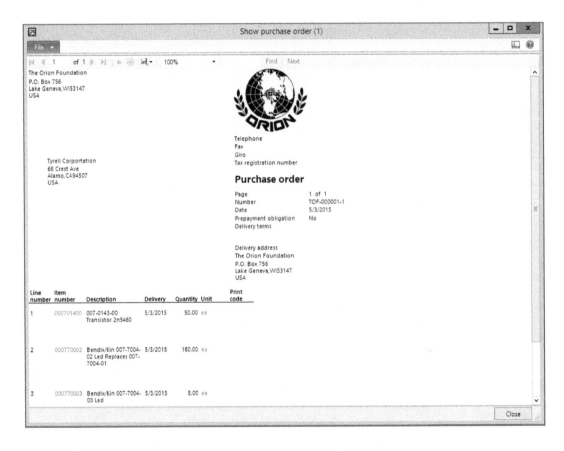

After a few seconds, the **Purchase Order Confirmation** will be displayed.

Note: You don't always have to have this printed to screen. You can use the **Print Management** to automatically print the Purchase Order, or even e-mail the Purchase Order to the vendor. But right now, printing to the screen is good enough.

When you are done, click on the **Close** button to exit from the form.

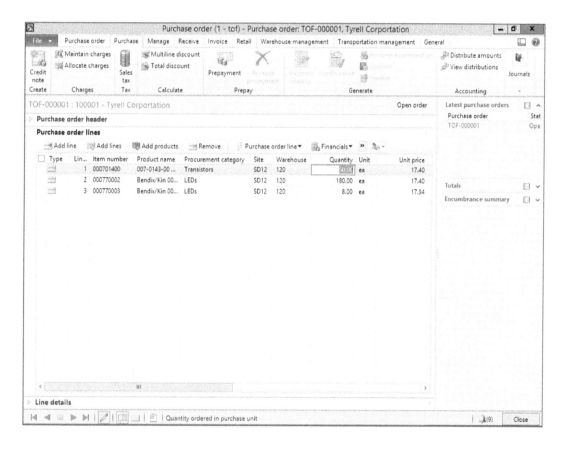

When you return to the **Purchase Order** you will see that all of the **Generate** buttons have been grayed out showing that you don't need to print the Confirmations.

Receiving In A Purchase Order

Once the **Purchase Order** has been confirmed you can receive it. There are a couple of different ways that the Purchase Orders can be received including through the handheld or through a Receiving Workbench, but you can also just receive it from the **Purchase Order** itself, and that is what we are going to do in this setp.

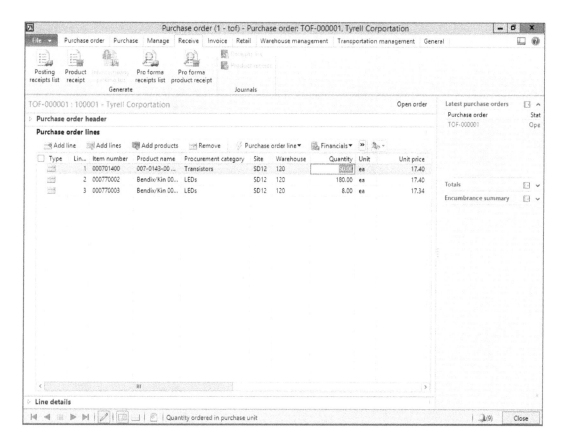

To receive the **Purchase Order**, just open the **Purchase Order Details** form and then click on the
Product Receipt button within the **Generate** group of the **Receive** ribbon bar.

146

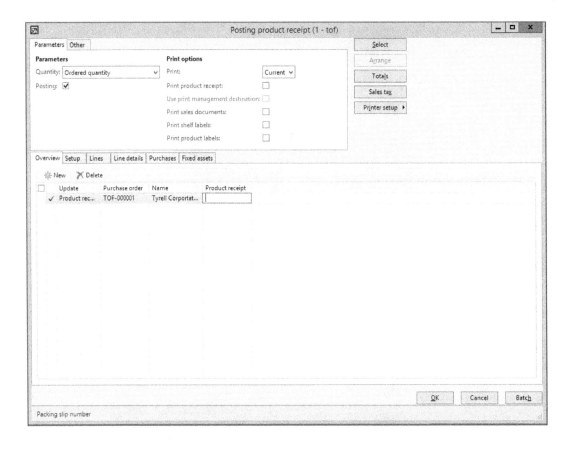

This will open up a **Purchase Order Receipt** maintenance form.

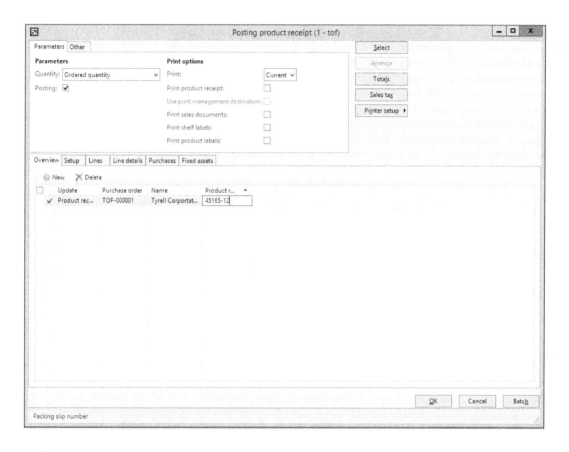

Start off by typing in the **Product Receipt** number for the receipt within the **Overview** tab.

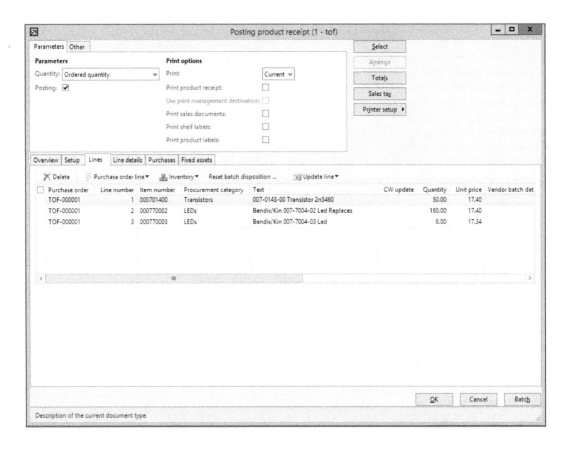

If you switch to the **Lines** tab you will be able to see all of the lines on the **Purchase Order** that are still waiting to be received in.

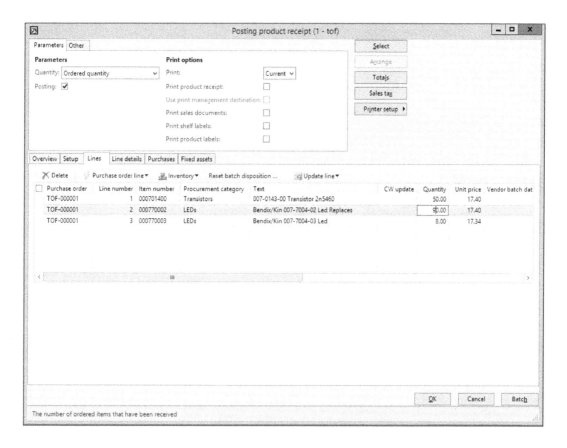

If you want to can select any of the lines and change the **Quantity** that you have received, to indicate over, or under shippments.

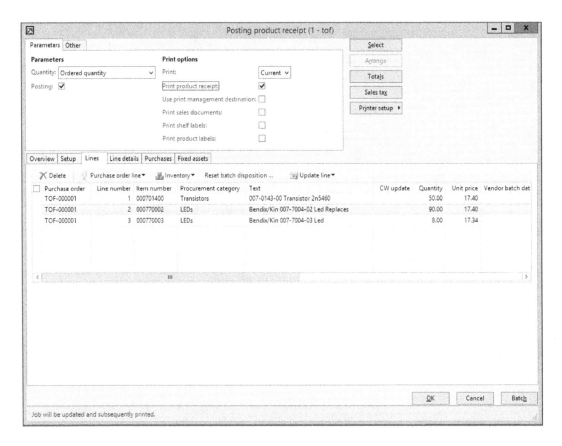

After you have updated the receipt, then just click on the **OK** button to receive in the products.

A Product Receipt summary document will be printed, and you can close out of that document.

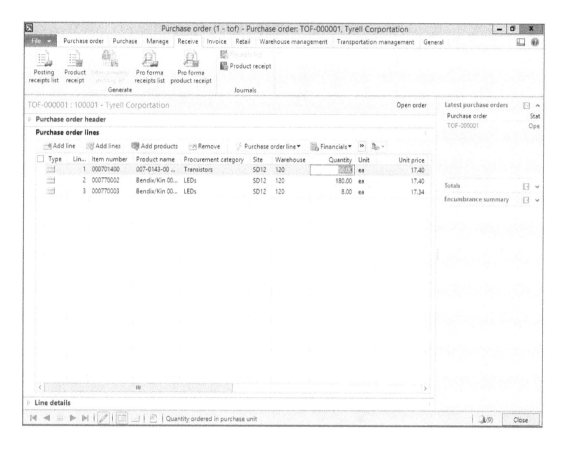

To receive the outstanding quantity, click on the **Product Receipt** button again within the
Generate group of the **Receive** ribbon bar.

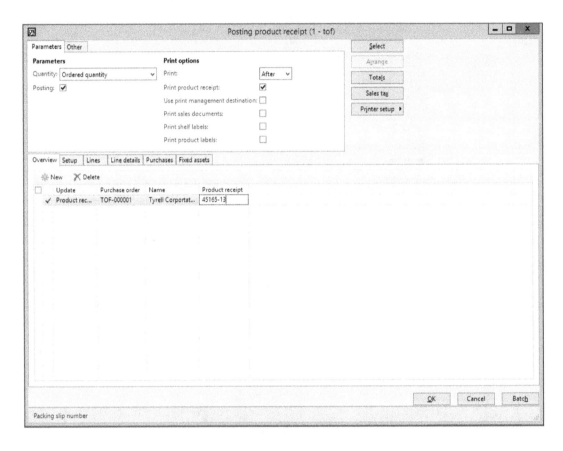

When the **Posting Product Receipt** dialog is displayed, enter in a new **Product Receipt** number.

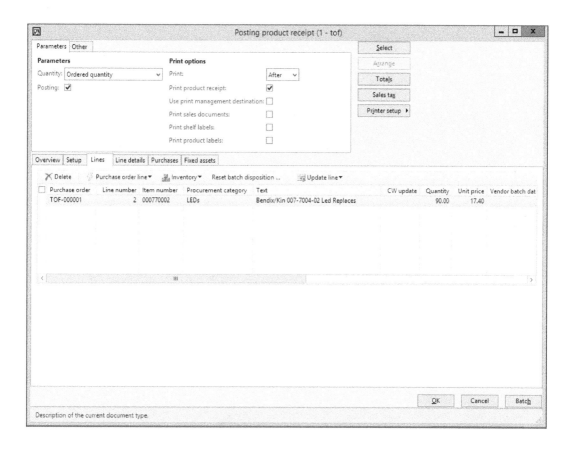

When you switch to the **Lines** you will notice that only the remaining quantity is being displayed.

All you need to do to receive the outstanding quantity is click on the **OK** button.

155

Reprinting Product Receipt Documents

If you want to reporting any of the receipt documents that were generated then you can quickly do that from the **Purchase Order**.

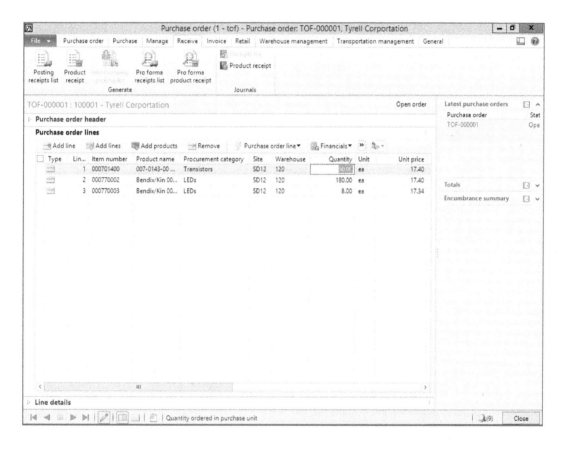

To do this just open up the **Purchase Order Details** form and click on the **Product Receipt** button within the **Journals** group of the **Receive** ribbon bar.

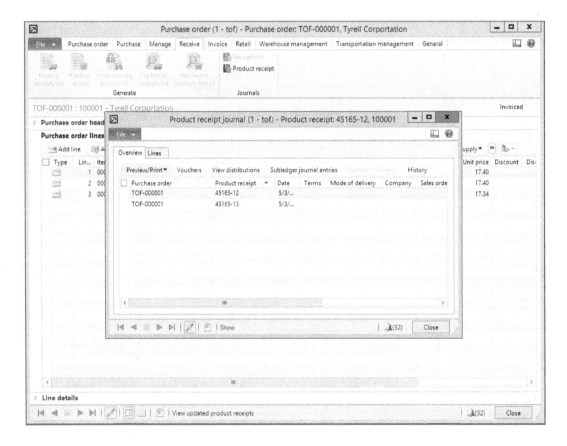

This will open up the **Product Receipt Journal** list showing all of the receipts that you have done for the **Purchase Order**.

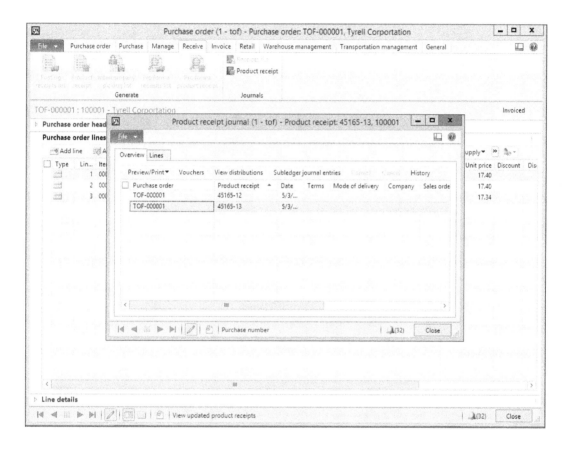

To reprint a particular receipts, just select **Receipt** line.

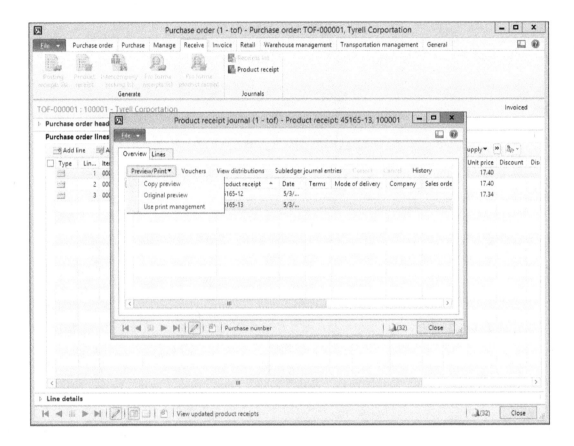

And then click on the **Print/Preview** menu item and select the **Original Preview** submenu item.

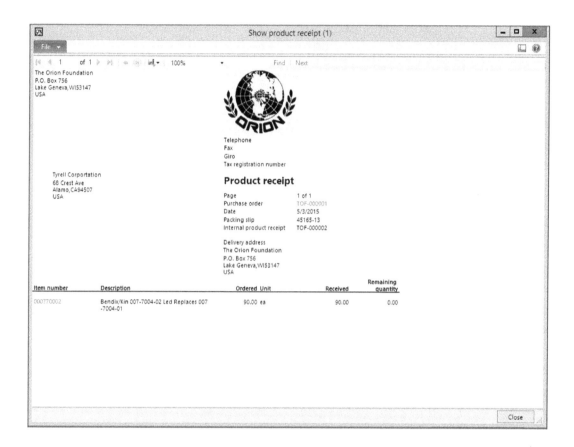

This will print out the **Product Receipt** document for you. From here you can e-mail, print, or save the document away.

When you are done, just click on the **Close** button to exit from the form.

Invoicing The Product Receipts

Once you have received against a Purchase Order, it is also ready to be Invoiced. You can do this in batch or you can do it directly from the **Purchase Order** which is what we will do in this example.

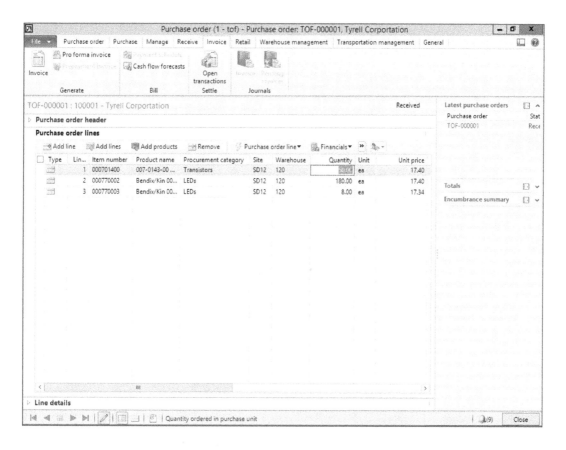

To create the **Invoice** from the **Purchase Order**, Open up the **Purchase Order Details** and then click on the **Invoice** button within the **Generate** group of the **Invoice** ribbon bar.

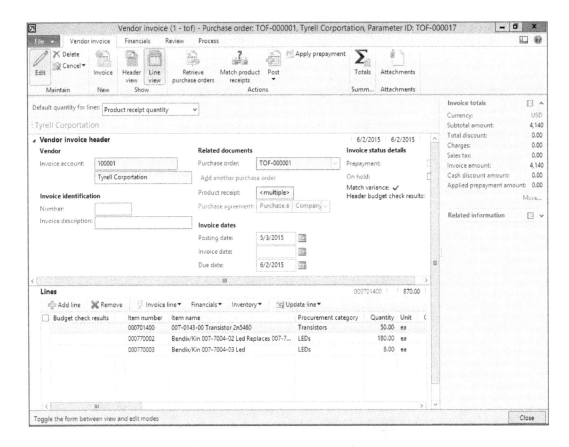

That will take all of the receipt information and covert it into an **Invoice** for you and also take you to the **Vendor Invoice** form.

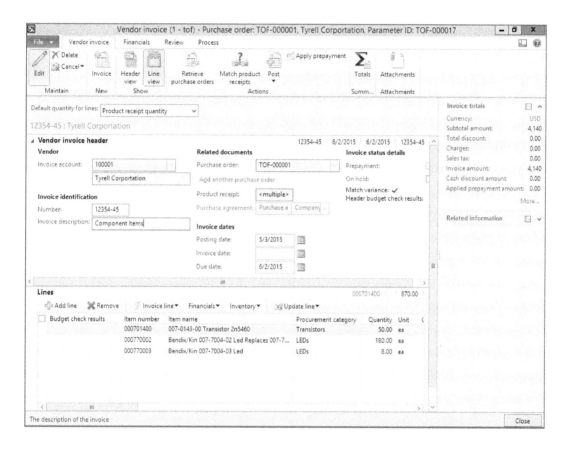

All you need to do is enter in the Vendors Invoice Number into the **Number** field, and if you want to you can also include an **Invoice Description.**

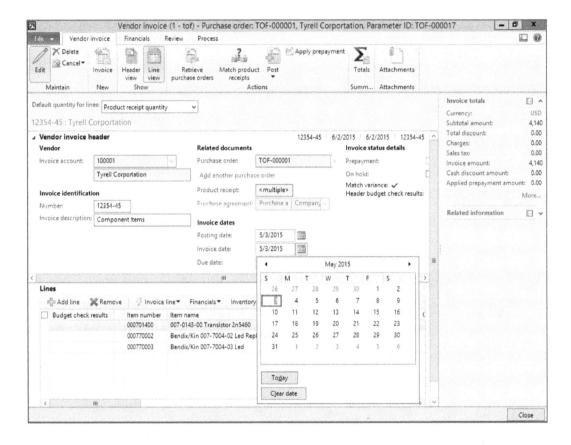

Next, click on the **Invoice Date** dropdown list and select the date that you want to record against the invoice – this will impact the due date that is calculated based on the Vendor Terms.

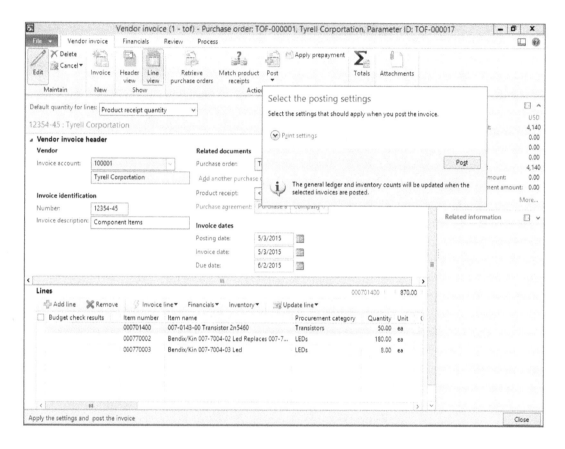

Once you have done that you can post the invoice to Payables by clicking on the **Post** button within the **Actions** group of the **Vendor Invoices** ribbon bar.

When the **Select the posting Settings** dialog box is displayed, just click on the **Post** button.

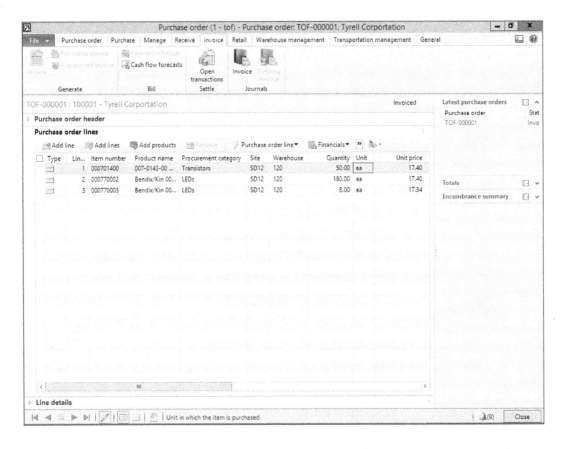

When you return back to the **Purchase Order** you will see that the Generate options are all grayed out because you don't have any more receipts that need to be invoiced.

Reprinting Vendor Invoices

Once the Purchase Order has been invoiced, you can always access the Invoice Journals and reprint any of the documentation.

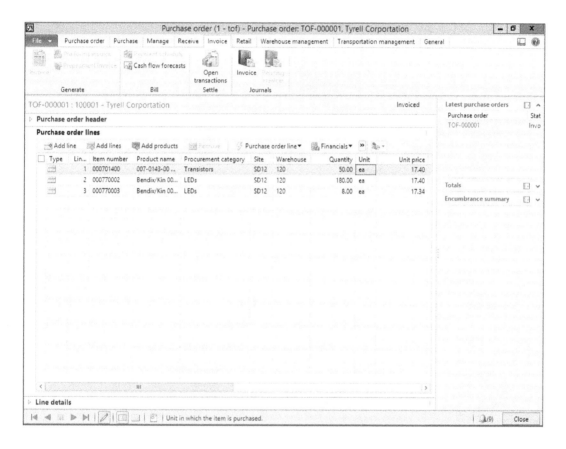

To do this, open up the **Purchase Order Details** and click on the **Invoices** button within the
Journals group of the **Invoice** ribbon bar.

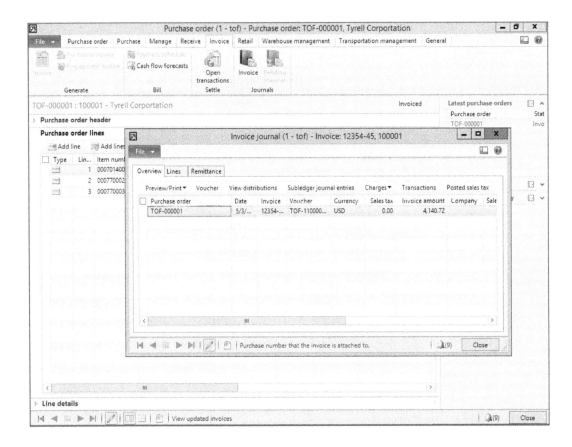

This will open up the **Invoice Journals** list, and you will be able to see all of the Invoices that are associated with the **Purchase Order**.

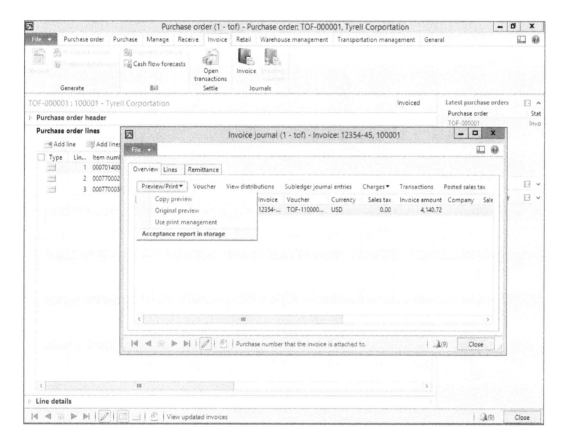

To reprint the Invoice just select the Invoice record, click on the **Print/Preview** menu item and select the **Original Preview** submenu item.

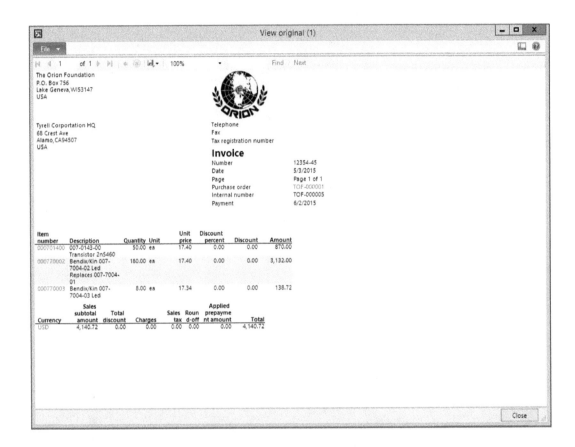

This will print out a copy of the **Vendor Invoice** for you. When you are done, just click on the **Close** button.

Viewing The Vendor Invoices Within Payables

You don't have to access the **Vendor Invoice** details from the **Procurement and Sourcing** area though, because all of the invoice information is automatically available to the **Accounts Payable** users as well.

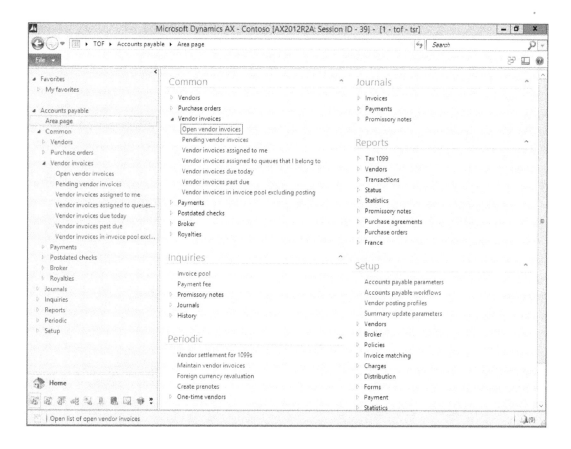

To view the Invoices there, click on the **Open Vendor Invoices** menu item within the **Vendor Invoices** folder of the **Common** group within the **Accounts Payable** area page.

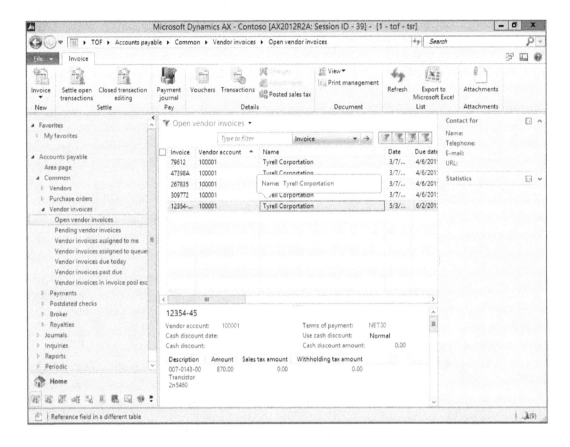

When the **Open Vendor Invoices** list page is displayed, you will be able to see the invoice that you just created through the **Procurement and Sourcing** area.

How efficient is that?

Viewing Inventory Transactions

Just as one final check to prove that everything is working correctly for the Purchase Order Receipt, you can also see the receipt transaction within the **Inventory Management** area.

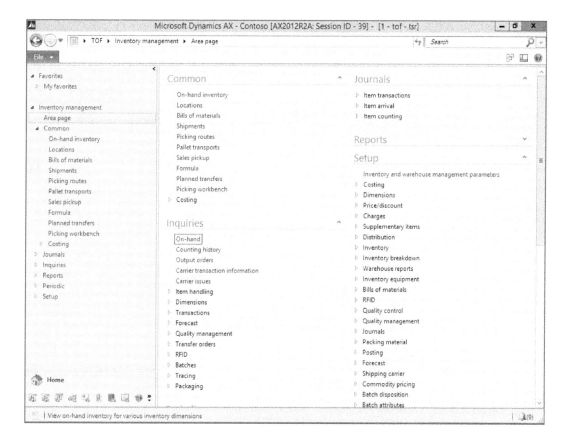

To view the inventory receipt details, click on the **On-Hand** menu item within the **Inquiries** group of the **Inventory Management** area page.

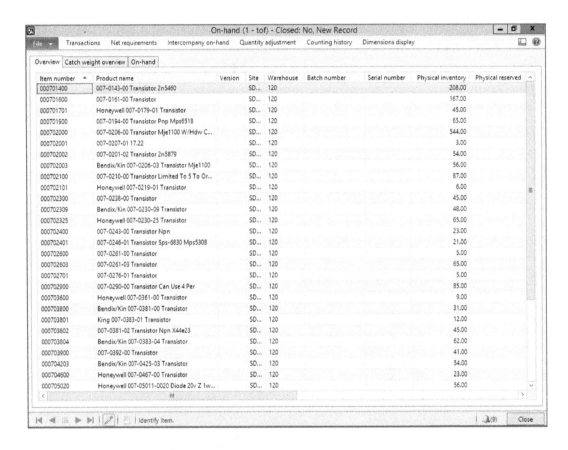

When the **On-Hand** inquiry is displayed, select any of the items that you received inventory against, and then click on the **Transactions** button within the menu bar.

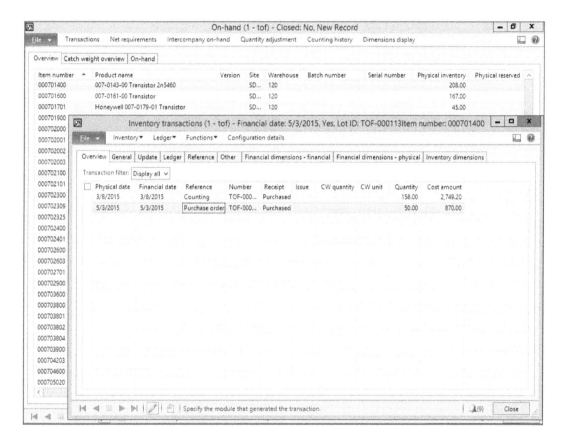

This will open up the **Inventory Transactions** list for that item and you will be able to see that there is a record there for the **Purchase Order Receipt**.

When you are done you can click the **Close** button to exit from the forms.

CONFIGURING PRICE LISTS & DISCOUNTS

Up until now, all of the prices that have been used as the Purchase Orders have been created have defaulted directly from the **Purchase Price** on the Released Product record. But that is not the only way that the prices can be configured. You can use the **Trade Agreements** feature within Dynamics AX to create price lists, customer price agreements, and also discount agreements that will automatically be used within the Purchase Orders.

In this section we will show you how you can use the **Trade Agreements** to manage all of you pricing and discounting requirements.

Activating Price Lists & Discounts

Before we start, there is a very important step that we need to perform, and that is to enable the pricing and discount agreements to be used within you Purchase Orders.

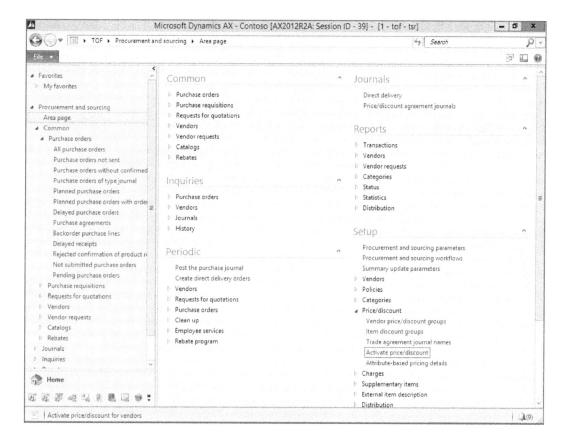

To do this, click on the **Activate Price/Discount** menu item within the **Price/Discount** folder of the **Setup** group within the **Procurement and Sourcing** area page.

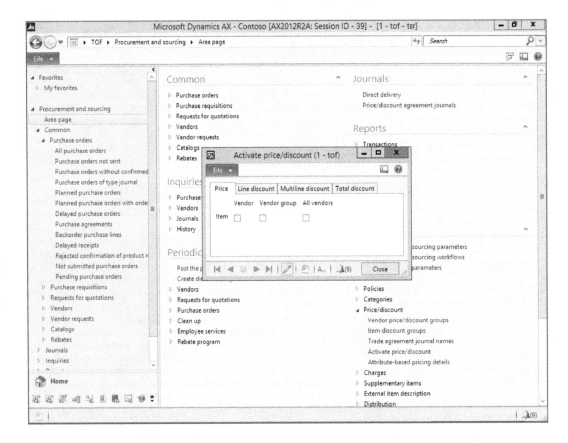

This will open up the **Activate Price/Discount** dialog box. This allows you to pick and choose what types of pricing and discounts will be recognized by the Procurement and Sourcing area within Dynamics AX.

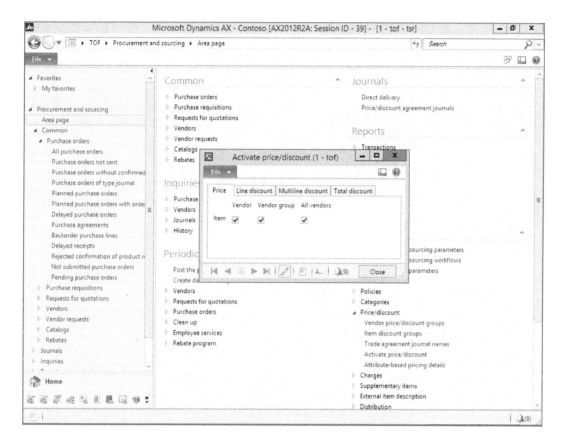

Start off on the **Pricing** tab. This is set up in a grid showing all of the Item combinations that are allowed down the left hand side, and also all of the **Vendor** combinations along the top. In this tab it is saying that Prices are only set at the **Item** level, but they can apply to just a **Vendor,** a **Vendor Group**, or apply to all **Vendors**. This is important to note because this means that you cannot set up a price list for a group of **Items** or a single price for **All Items**.

We want to enable all types of allowed pricing so check all of the options.

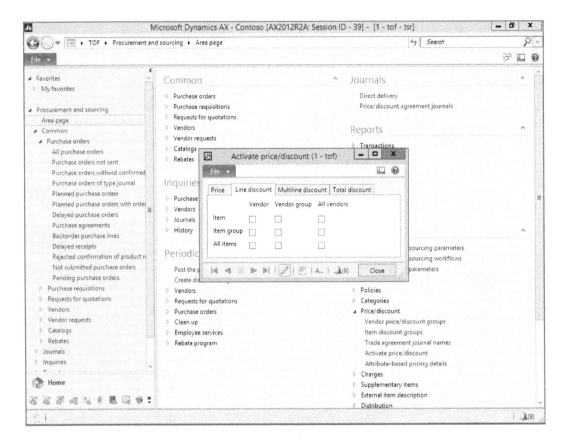

Next switch to the **Line Discount** tab. Here you will see that you have more **Item** options, so we can allow discounts for one, a group, or all **Vendors**, and also for one, a group, or all **Items**, with all combinations allowed.

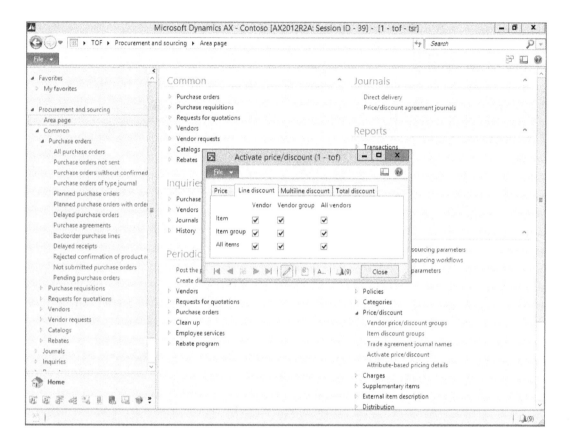

We want to enable all types of allowed pricing so check all of the options.

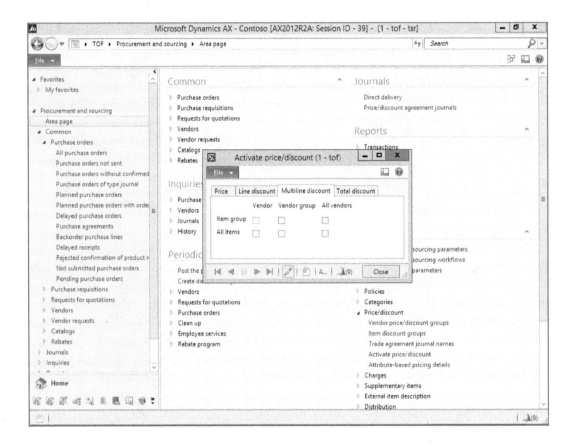

Next we will switch to the **Multiline Discounts** tab. This allows us to define discounts that apply to multiple lines within the purchase order, allowing for cumulative discounts based on multiple line items. Here we can allow discounts for one, a group, or all **Vendors**, and but only for a group, or all **Items** which makes sense because you should only have one line already for an item.

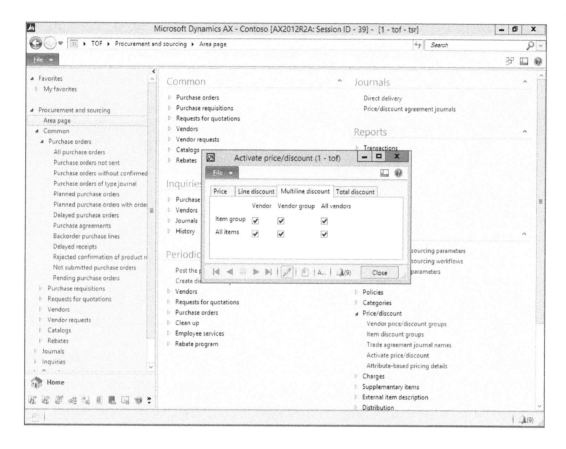

We want to enable all types of allowed pricing so check all of the options.

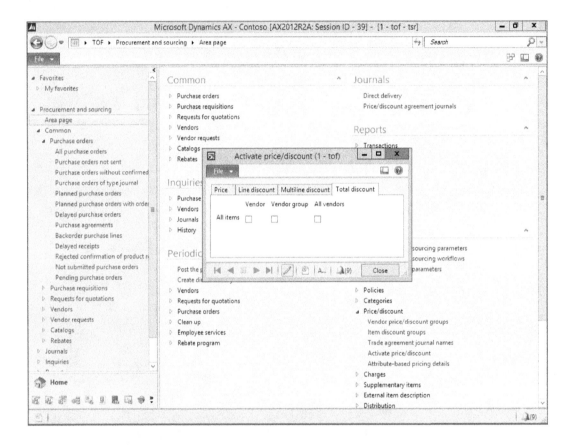

Finally we will switch to the **Total Discounts** tab. This allows us to define discounts that apply to purchase order in general at the header level. Here we can allow discounts for one, a group, or all **Vendors**, and but only for all **Items** because there are no items on the Purchase Order Header.

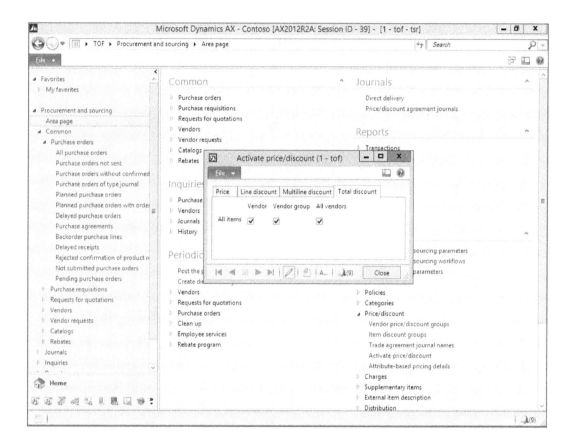

We want to enable all types of allowed pricing so check all of the options.

When you have done this click on the **Close** button to exit from the form.

Creating Vendor Price/Discount Groups

Before we start creating our **Trade Agreements** we will want to set up some more codes. The first one that we will set up will be the **Vendor Price/Discount Groups**. These will be assigned to the **Vendors** themselves to allow us to group them for our **Prices** and **Discounts**, allowing us to create single agreements that apply to multiple vendors, saving us from having to create the same trade agreement for each **Vendor**.

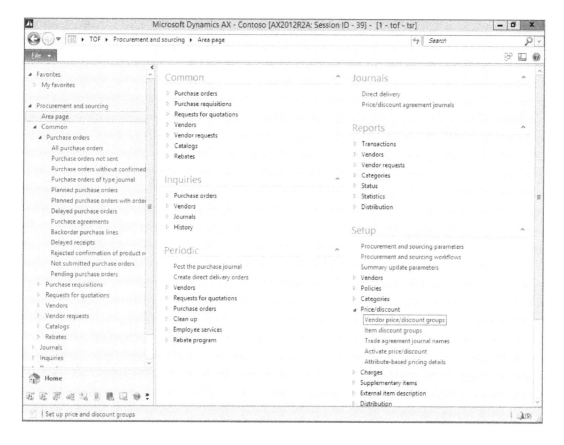

To do this, click on the **Vendor Price/Discount Groups** menu item within the **Price/Discount** folder of the **Setup** group of the **Procurement and Sourcing** area page.

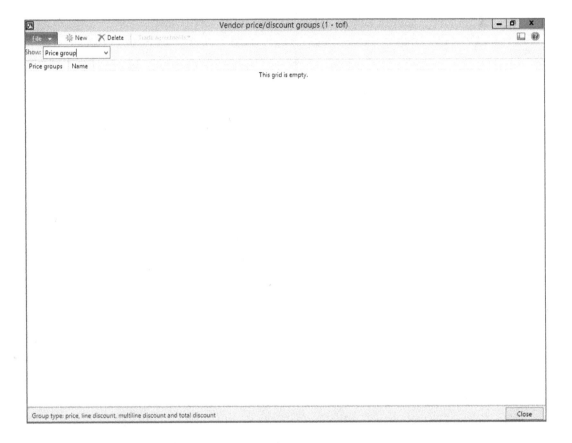

This will open up the **Vendor Price/Discount Groups** maintenance form. Initially the **Show** field will be set to the **Price Group** option indicating that we will be setting up Price Groups.

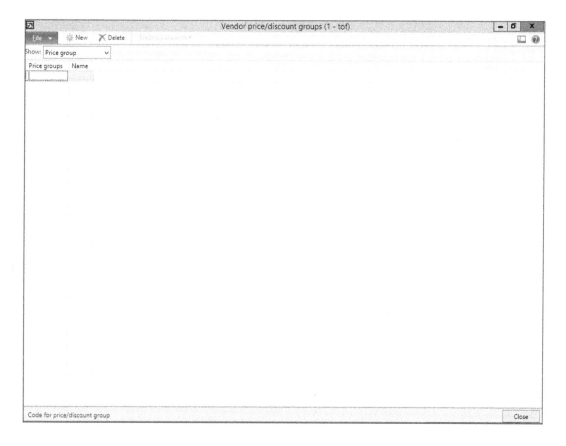

Click on the **New** button in the menu bar to create a new record.

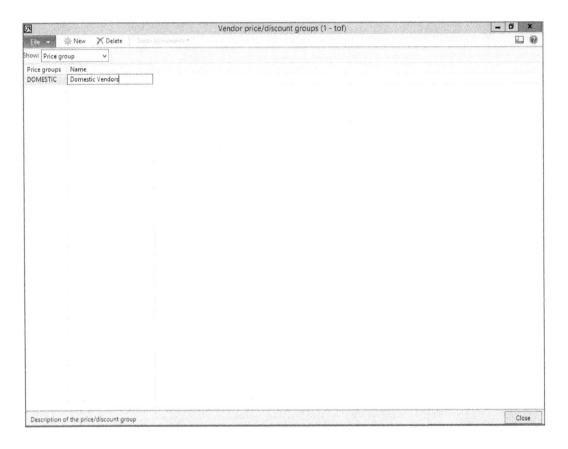

Then set the **Price Group** code to **DOMESTIC** and the **Name** to **Domestic Vendors**.

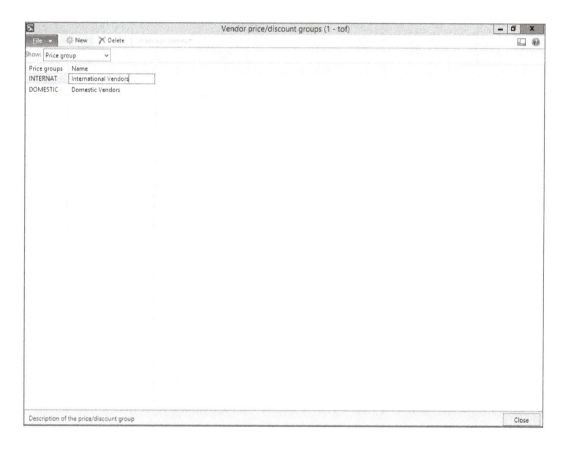

Click on the **New** button in the menu bar to create a new record and then set the **Price Group** code to **INTERNAT** and the **Name** to **International Vendors**.

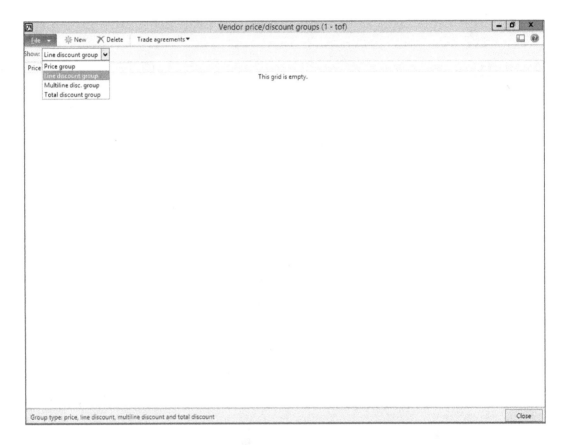

Now click on the **Show** dropdown list and you will see all of the other types of **Price/Discount Groups** that we can set up here. Select the **Line Discount Group** option to set up some Vendor groupings for the Line Discounts.

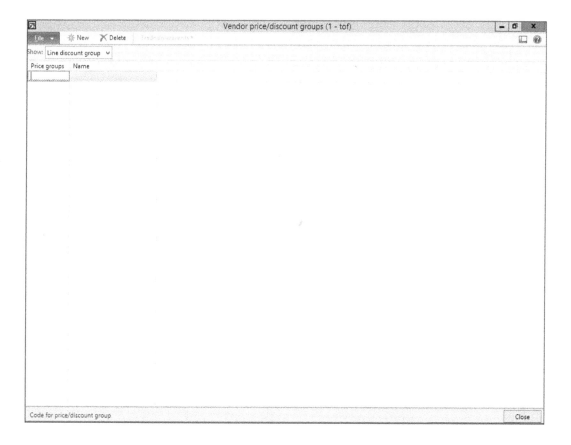

When the **Vendor Price/Discount Groups** table refreshed, click on the **New** button in the menu bar to create a new record.

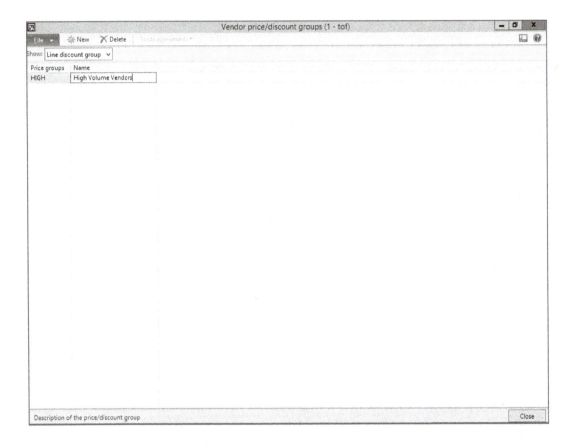

Then set the **Price Group** code to **HIGH** and the **Name** to **High Volume Vendors**.

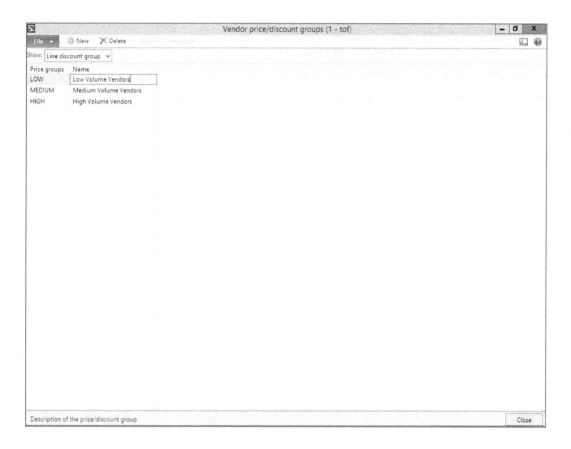

Then repeat the process to add the following **Price Groups**:

Price Group	Name
LOW	Low Volume Vendors
MEDIUM	Medium Volume Vendors

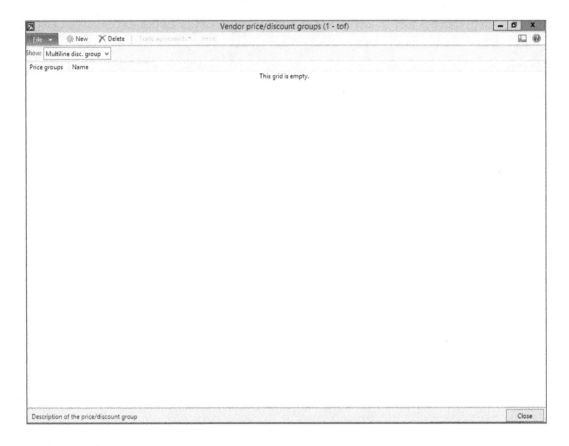

Now click on the **Show** dropdown list and select the **Multiline Discount Group** option to set up some Vendor groupings for the Multiline Discounts.

When the **Vendor Price/Discount Groups** table refreshed, click on the **New** button in the menu bar to create a new record.

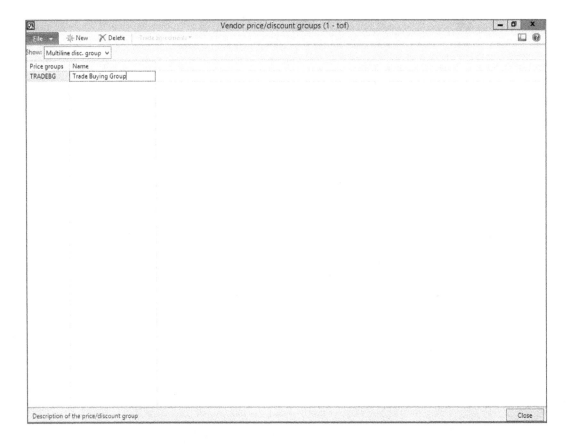

Then set the **Price Group** code to **TRADEBG** and the **Name** to **Trade Buying Group**.

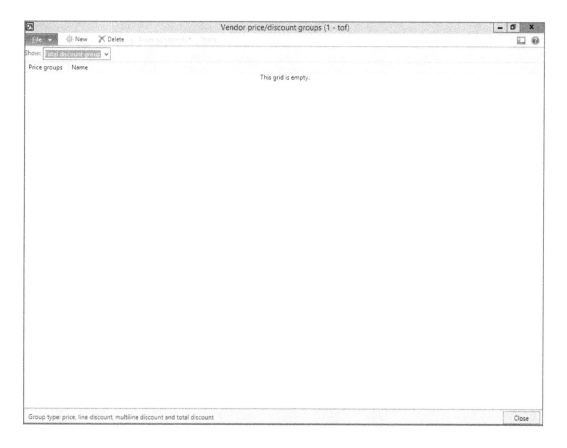

Now click on the **Show** dropdown list and select the **Total Discount Group** option to set up some Vendor groupings for the Total Order Discounts.

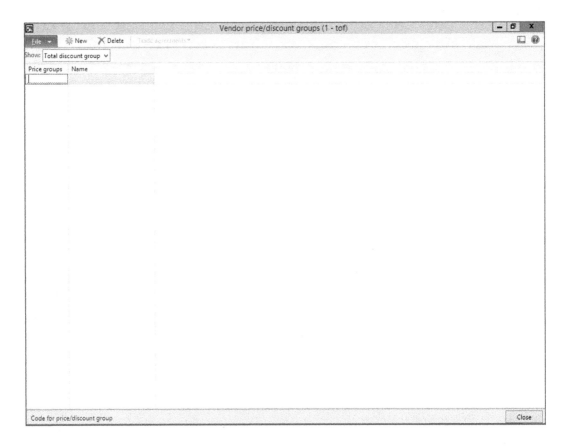

When the **Vendor Price/Discount Groups** table refreshed, click on the **New** button in the menu bar to create a new record.

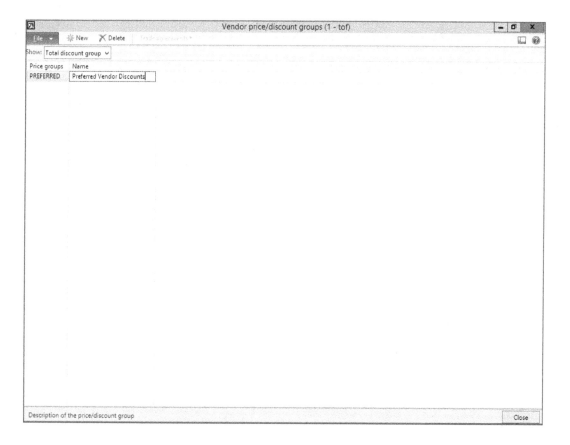

Then set the **Price Group** code to **PREFERRED** and the **Name** to **Preferred Vendor Discounts**.

And click on the **New** button in the menu bar to create a new record and set the **Price Group** code to **STANDARD** and the **Name** to **Standard Vendor Discounts**.

Configuring Vendor Purchasing Defaults

Now that we have the Vendor Price and Discount Groups configured we will want to assign them to our **Vendors** records, and also while we are here we will add a few more default values to streamline the purchasing process.

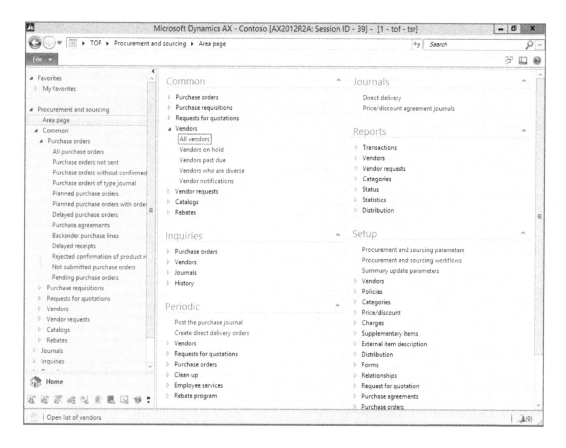

To do this, click on the **All Vendors** menu item within the **Vendors** folder of the **Common** group within the **Procurement and Sourcing** area page.

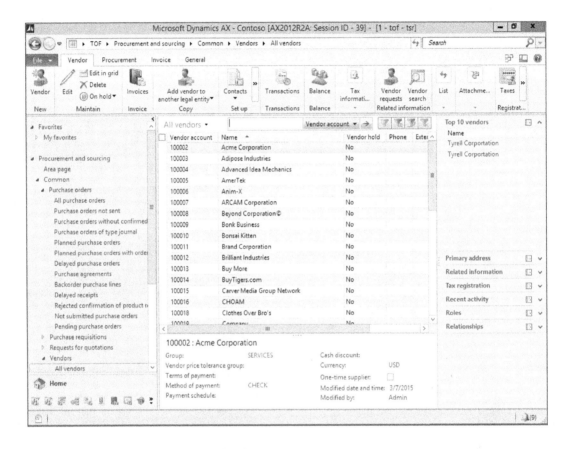

When the **All Vendors** list page is displayed, select the vendor record that you want to update and then click on the **Edit** button within the **Maintain** group of the **Vendor** ribbon bar.

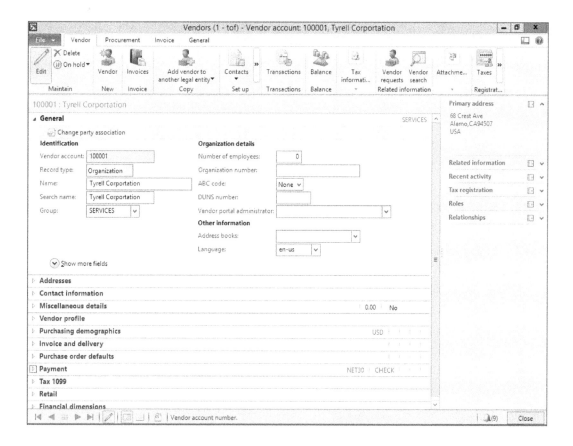

This will open up the **Vendor Details** form.

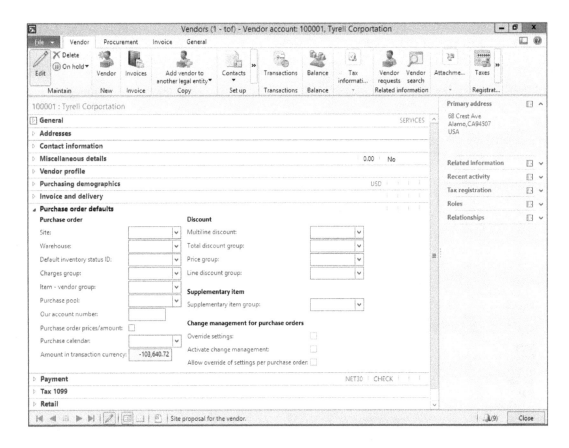

Open up the **Purchase Order Defaults** tab and you will see that there are a few codes here that you can default in during the purchasing process.

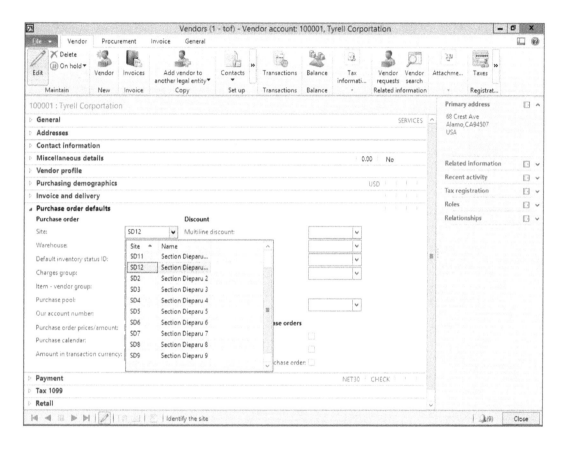

Start off by clicking on the **Site** dropdown list and you will see all of your sites are listed here. Select the **Site** that you want to automatically default in for this vendor when you create the Purchase Order. In this example we will choose **SD12**.

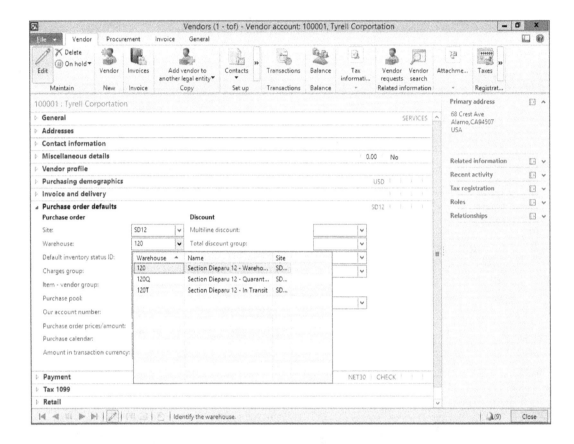

Then click on the **Warehouse** dropdown list and you will see all of the default Sites Warehouses are listed here. Select the **Warehouse** that you want to automatically default in for this vendor when you create the Purchase Order. In this example we will choose **120**.

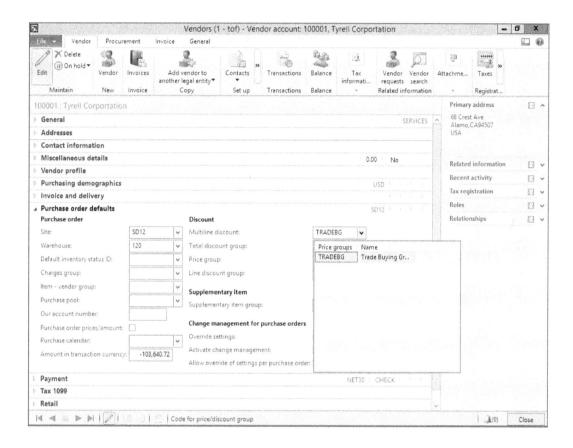

Now click on the **Multiline Discount** dropdown list. This will list all of the Mutiline Discounts that you just configured. Select the one that you want to use for the Vendor – in this case **TRADEBG**.

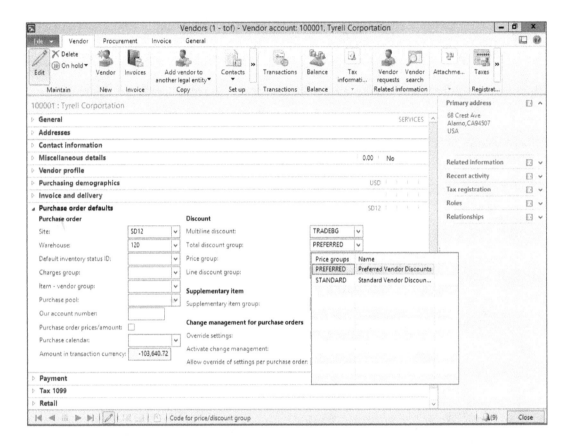

Now click on the **Total Discount Group** dropdown list. This will list all of the Total Discounts Groups that you just configured. Select the one that you want to use for the Vendor – in this case **PREFERRED**.

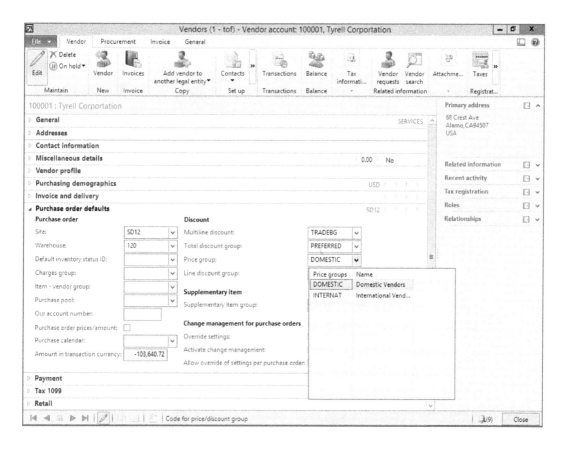

Now click on the **Price Group** dropdown list. This will list all of the Price Groups that you just configured. Select the one that you want to use for the Vendor – in this case **DOMESTIC**.

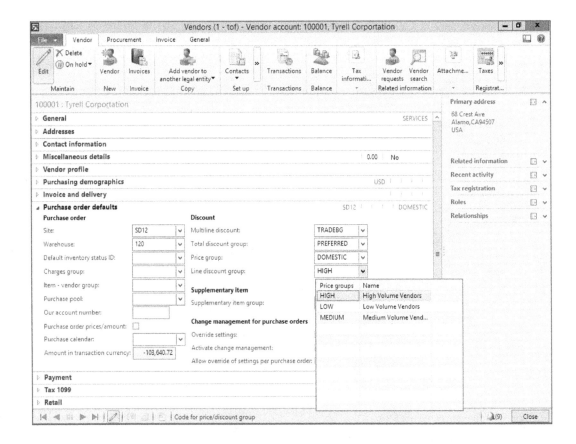

Now click on the **Line Discount Group** dropdown list. This will list all of the Line Discount Groups that you just configured. Select the one that you want to use for the Vendor – in this case **HIGH**.

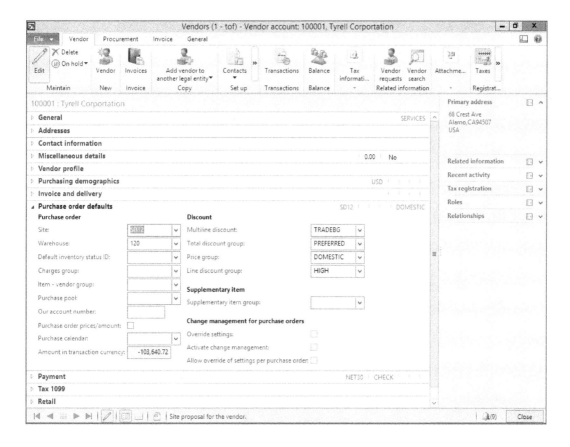

After you have done that you can update any other records you need to and when you are finished, click on the **Close** button to exit from the form.

Configuring Item Discount Groups

Now we will repeat the process for the **Item Discount Groupings** to allow us to group them for our **Discounts** for **Items**.

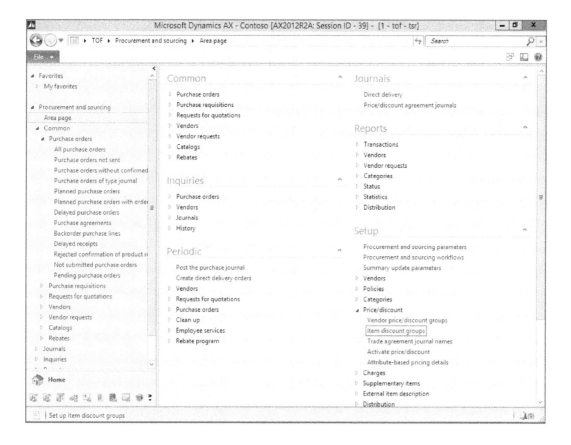

To do this, click on the **Item Discount Groups** menu item within the **Price/Discount** folder of the **Setup** group within the **Procurement and Sourcing** area page.

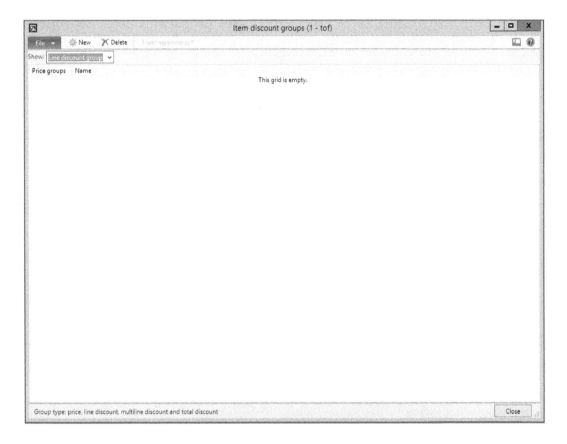

This will open up the **Item Discount Groups** maintenance form. Initially the **Show** field will be set to the **Line Discount Group** option indicating that we will be setting up Line Discounts.

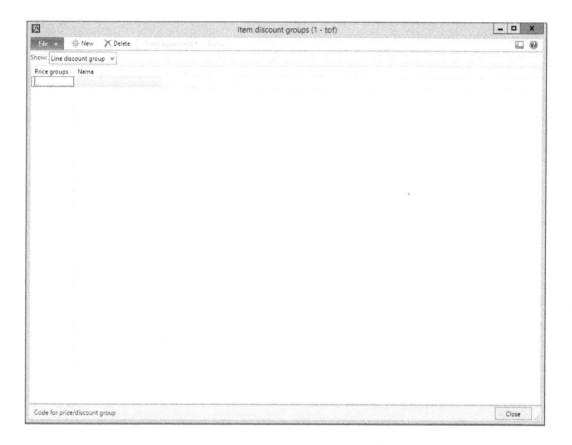

Click on the **New** button in the menu bar to create a new record.

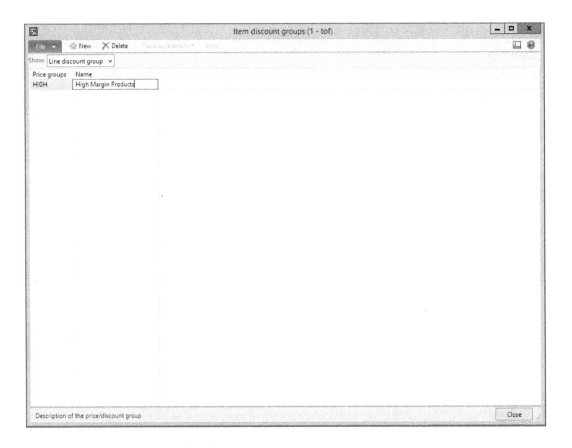

Then set the **Price Group** code to **HIGH** and the **Name** to **High Margin Products**.

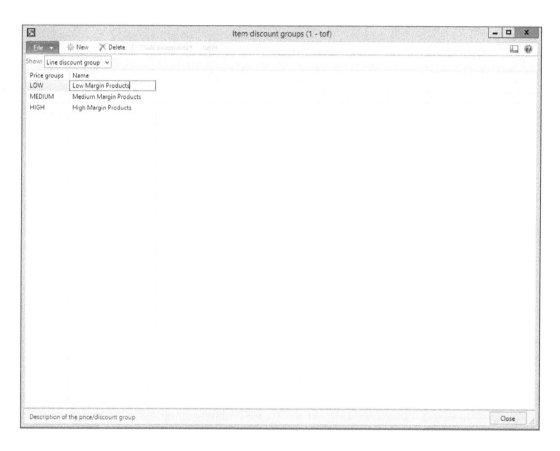

Then repeat the process to add the following **Price Groups**:

Price Group	Name
LOW	Low Volume Products
MEDIUM	Medium Volume Products

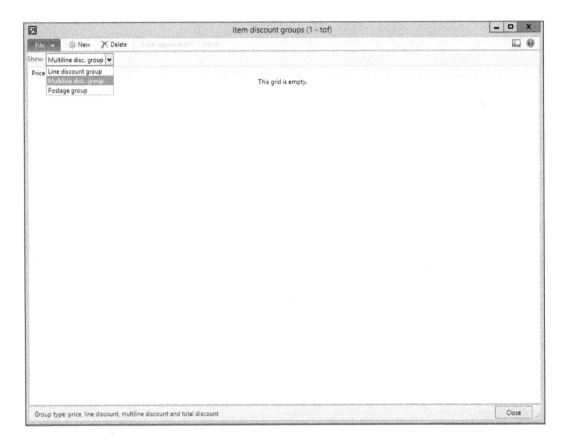

Now click on the **Show** dropdown list and select the **Multiline Discount Group** option to set up some Item groupings for the Multiline Discounts.

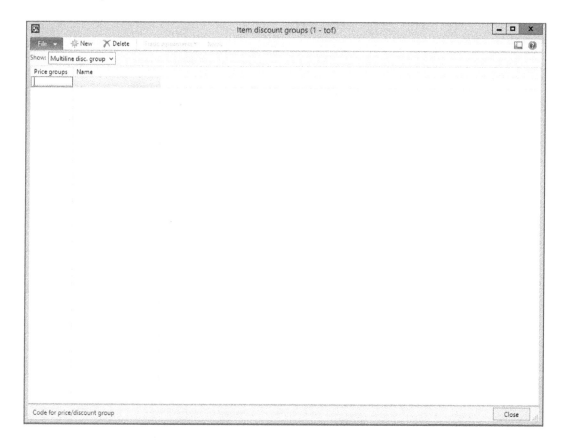

Click on the **New** button in the menu bar to create a new record.

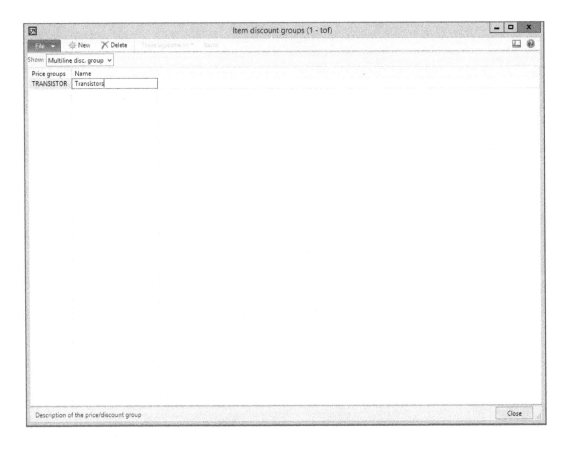

Then set the **Price Group** code to **TRANSISTOR** and the **Name** to **Transistors**.

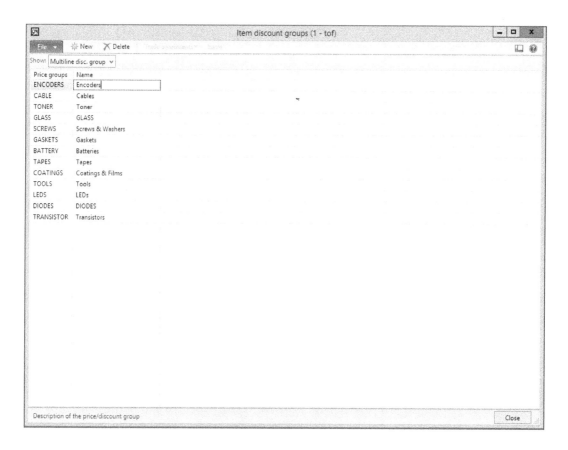

Then repeat the process to add the following **Price Groups**:

Price Group	Name	Price Group	Name
ENCODERS	Encoders	BATTERY	Batteries
CABLE	Cables	TAPES	Tapes
TONER	Toner	COATINGS	Coatings
GLASS	Glass	TOOLS	Tools
SCREWS	Screws	LEDS	LEDs
GASKETS	Gaskets	DIODES	Diodes

When you are done, click the **Close** button to exit from the form.

Configuring The Product Purchasing Defaults

Now that we have the Item Discount Groups configured we will want to assign them to add them to our **Items** records, and also while we are here we will add a few more default values to streamline the purchasing process.

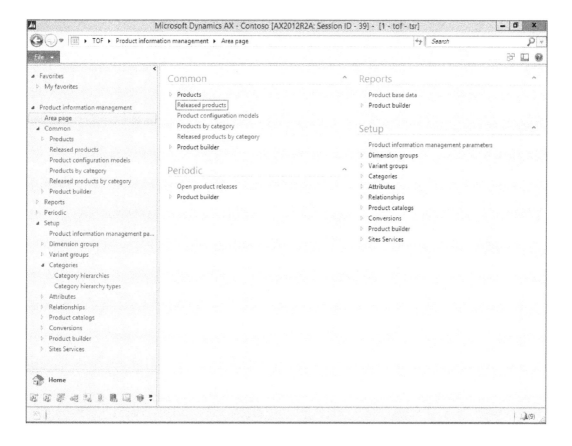

To do this click on the **Release Products** menu item within the **Common** group of the **Product Information Management** area page.

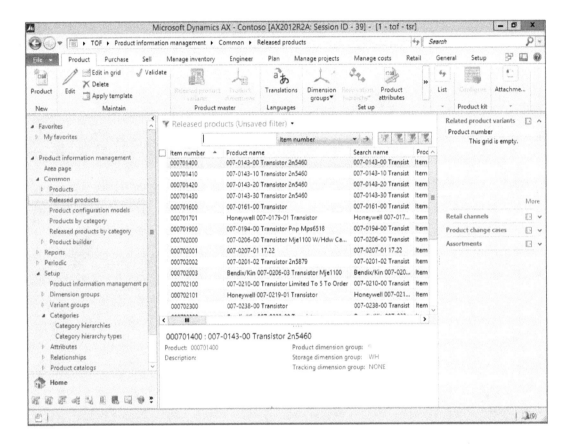

When the **Release Products** list page is displayed, select the released product record that you want to update and then click on the **Edit** button within the **Maintain** group of the **Product** ribbon bar.

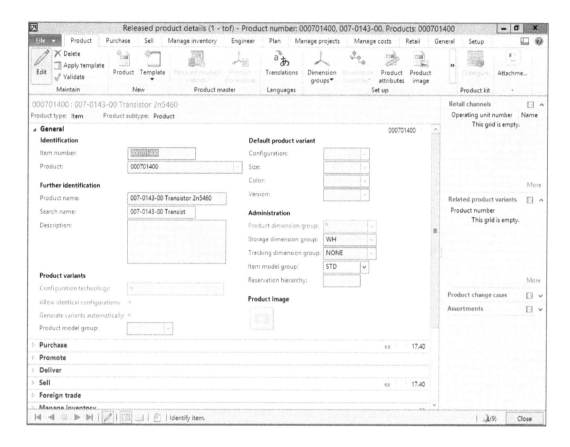

This will open up the **Released Product Details** page/

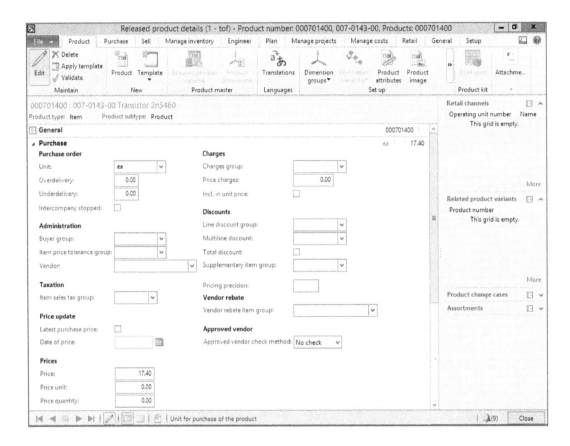

Open up the **Purchase Order Defaults** tab and you will see that there are a few codes here that you can default in during the purchasing process.

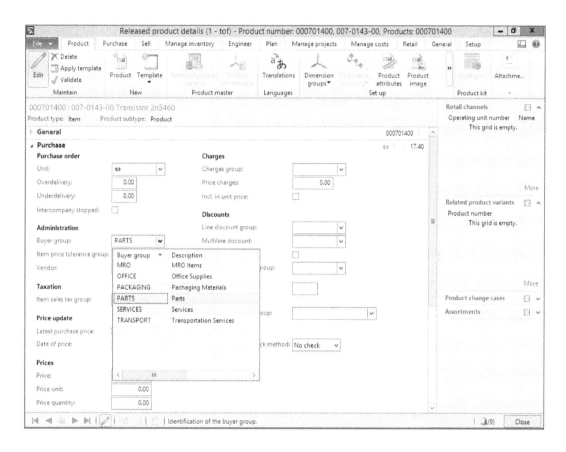

Start off by clicking on the **Buyer Group** field dropdown list and selecting a **Buyer Group** for this item. In this example we will assign it to the **Parts** Buyer Group.

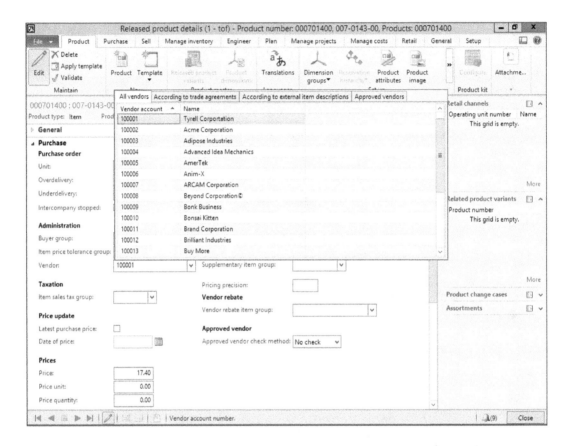

Then click on the **Vendor** dropdown list and select the default vendor that you will be purchasing the product from. This does not stop you from buying the product from anyone else, it does though mean that you don't have to type in a vendor whenever the system suggests a purchase order.

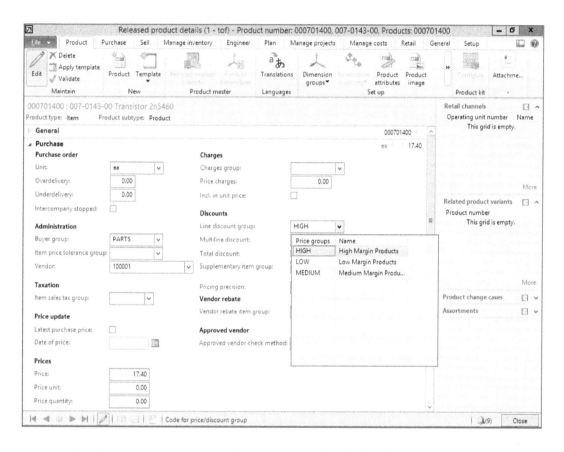

Now click on the **Line Discount Group** dropdown list. This will list all of the Line Discount Groups that you just configured. Select the one that you want to use for the Item – in this case **HIGH**.

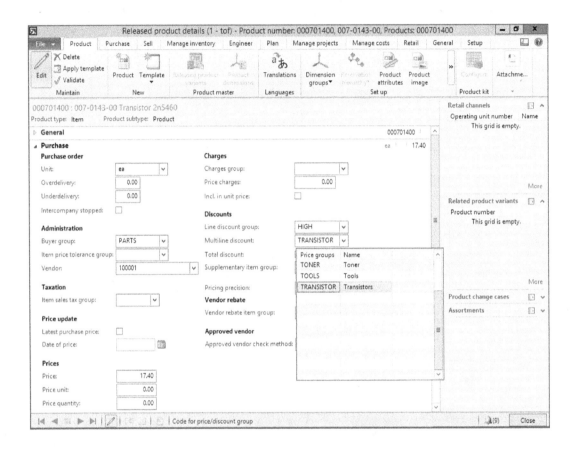

Now click on the **Multiline Discount** dropdown list. This will list all of the Multiline Discount Groups that you just configured. Select the one that you want to use for the Item – in this case **TRANSISTOR**.

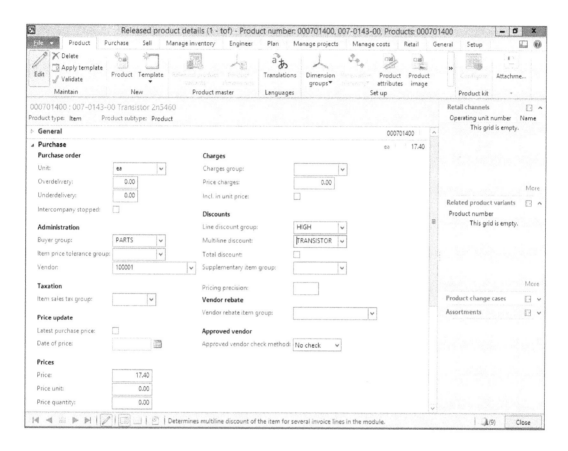

After you have done that you can update any other records you need to and when you are finished, click on the **Close** button to exit from the form.

Configuring Trade Agreement Journals

There is one final step that we need to perform and that is to set up some **Trade Agreement Journals**. These are not like the other Journals that you have configured, they are just classifications for your trade agreements that allow you to segregate them out based on type, and also default in the type of trade agreement they are to save a little bit of time.

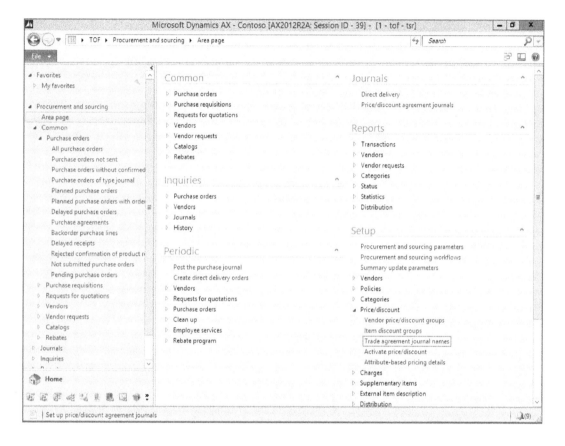

To do this, click on the **Trade Agreement Journal Names** menu item within the **Price/Discount** folder of the **Setup** group within the **Procurement and Sourcing** area page.

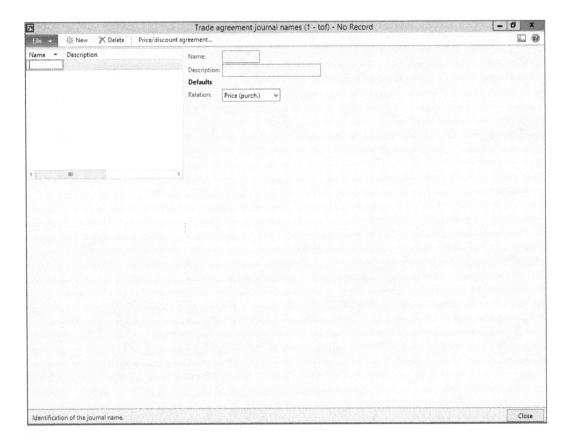

When the **Trade Agreement Journal Names** form is displayed, click on the **New** button in the menu bar to create a new record.

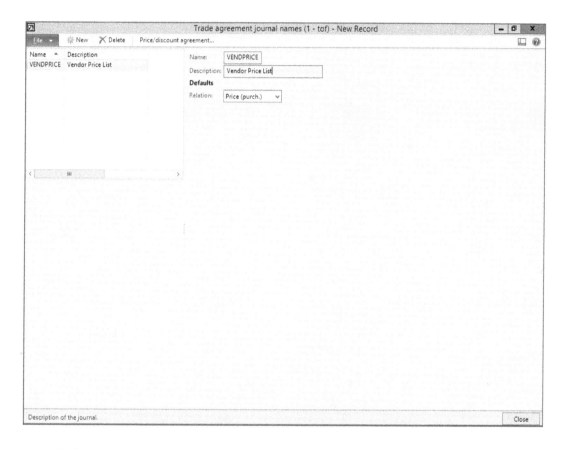

Set the first records **Name** to **VENDPRICE** and the **Description** to **Vendor List Price**.

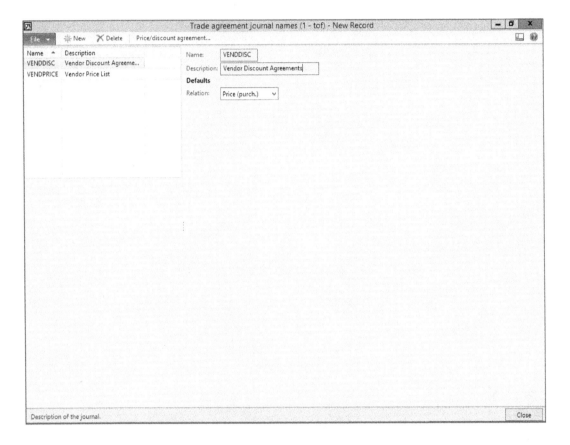

Then click on the **New** button in the menu bar to create a new record and set the **Name** to
VENDDISC and the **Description** to **Vendor Discount Agreements**.

For this record, click on the **Relation** dropdown list and change the value to **Line disc. (purch)** to indicate that this Trade Agreement is a Line Discount type.

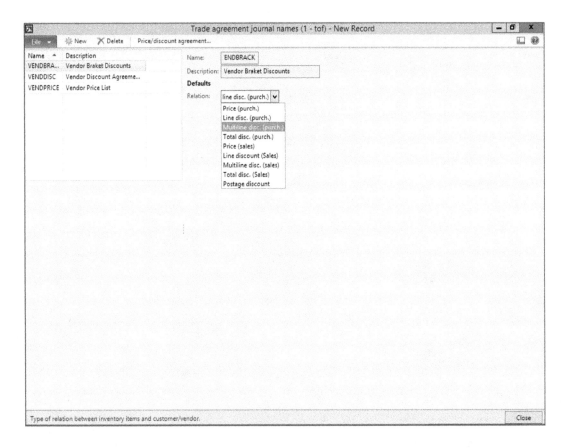

Then click on the **New** button in the menu bar to create a new record, set the **Name** to **VENDBRACK**, the **Description** to **Vendor Bracket Discounts**, and click on the **Relation** dropdown list and change the value to **Multiline disc. (purch)** to indicate that this Trade Agreement is a Multiline Discount type.

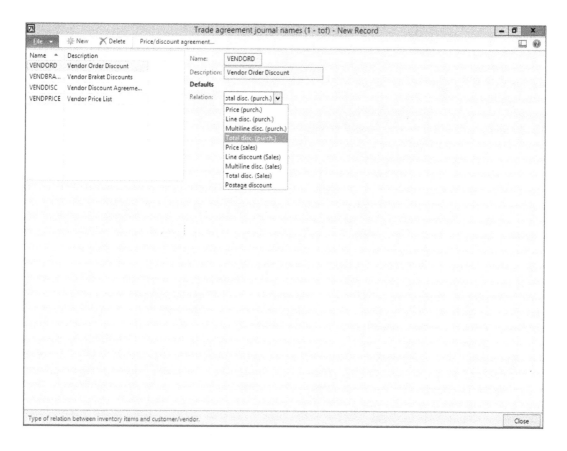

Finally click on the **New** button in the menu bar to create one last record, set the **Name** to **VENDORD**, the **Description** to **Vendor Order Discount**, and click on the **Relation** dropdown list and change the value to **Total disc. (purch)** to indicate that this Trade Agreement is a Order Discounts.

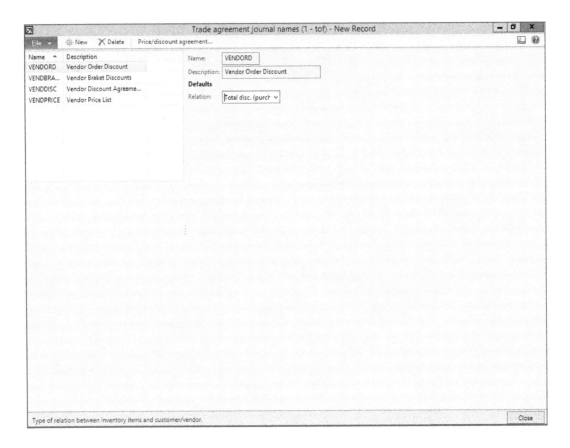

When you are done, just click on the **Close** button to exit from the form.

Creating A Vendor Price List

Now we can start creating our **Trade Agreements**. The first one that we will set up will be a simple Vendor Price list which lists out all of the agreed upon priced that you have negotiated with the vendors.

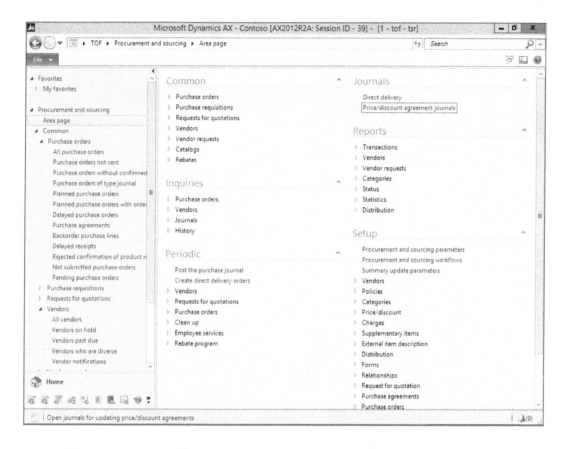

To do this, click on the **Price/Discount Agreement Journals** menu item within the **Journals** group of the **Procurement and Sourcing** area page.

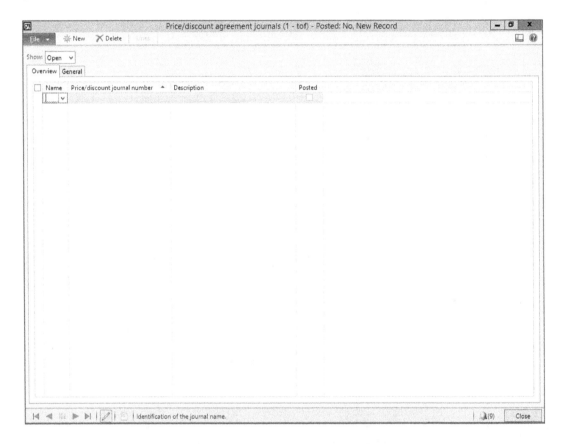

When the **Price/Discount Agreement Journals** maintenance form is displayed, click on the **New** button in the menu bar to create a new record.

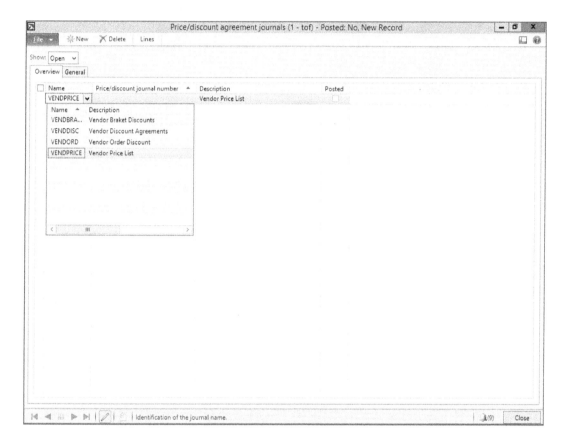

Then click on the **Name** dropdown list so that you can see all of the **Journal Names** that you
just created and select the **VENDPRICE** value.

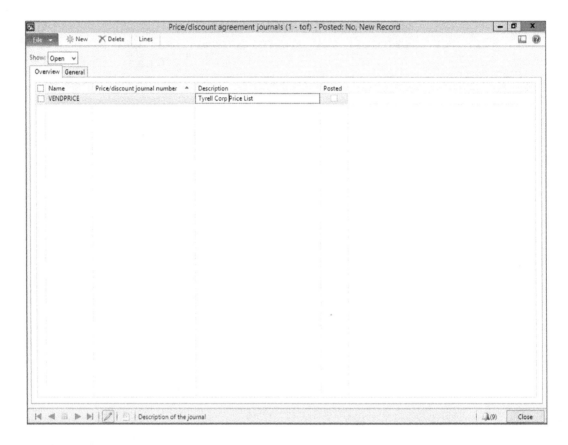

The **Description** will default in off the **Journal Type**, but you may want to change the name to make it easier to track down later on.

After you have done that click on the **Lines** button in the menu bar.

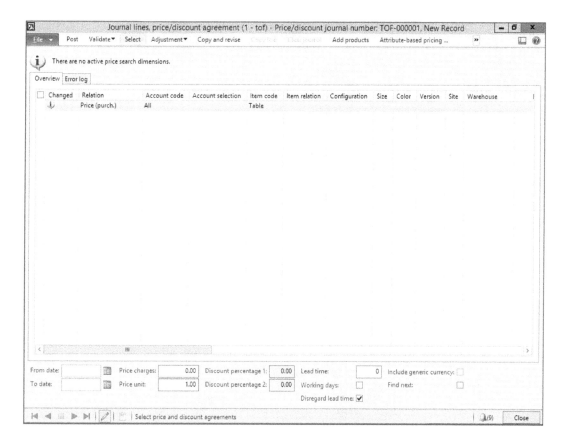

This will open up the **Journal Lines** maintenance form.

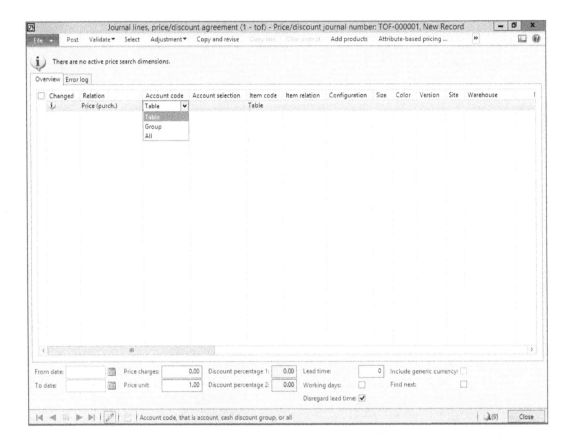

Click on the **Account Code** dropdown list. Here you will see three options that allow you to specify the vendor level that this trade agreement applies to. The **Table** option will allow you to say that it applies just to a single table record (i.e. a Vendor); the **Group** option will allow you to assign this price list to a Vendor Price Group, with multiple Vendors being assigned the price; and the **All** option will apply this price list to all vendors.

Select the **Table** option.

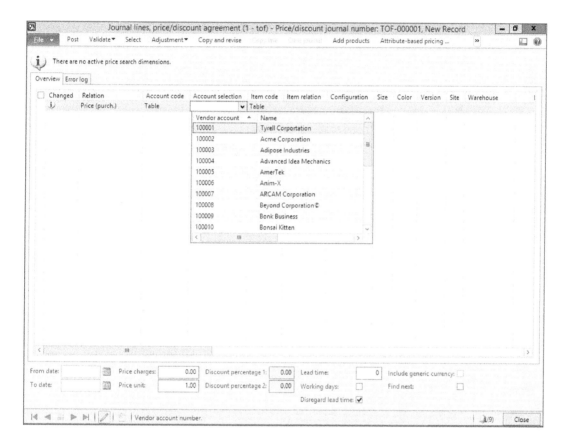

Now you can click on the **Account Selection** and you will see that all **Vendors** are listed. Select the **100001** vendor.

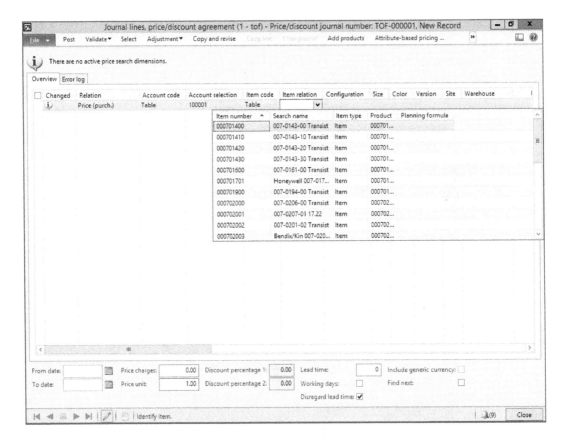

Now you can click on the **Item Relation** and you will see that all **Products** are listed, and you can select the one that you want to override the price for this vendor on. Select the **000701400** product.

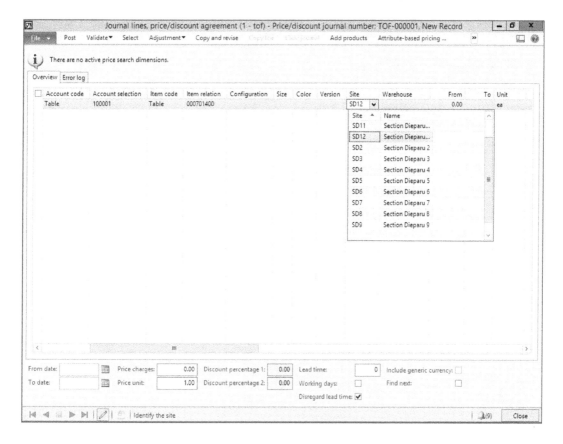

Next click on the **Site** dropdown and select the **Site** that you want this price to be applied to. In this case we select the **SD12** site.

Note: This is important, because each site could have it's own negotiated price with vendors.

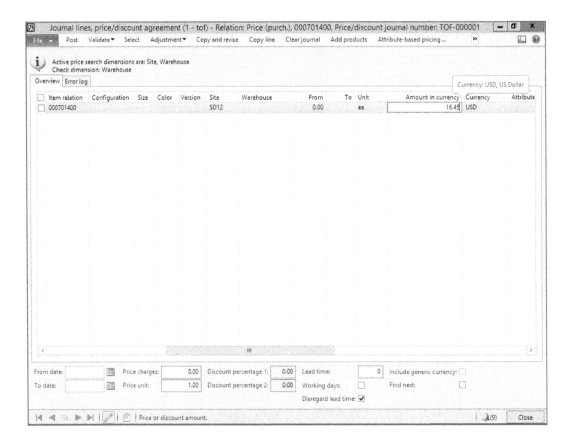

Finally, enter in the **Price** that you want to use for the product/vendor combination into the **Amount In Currency** field.

You can repeat this process and keep on adding more Item prices if you like.

Posting A Price List

Trade Agreements are not live until you post them. So the next step is to make them official and do just that.

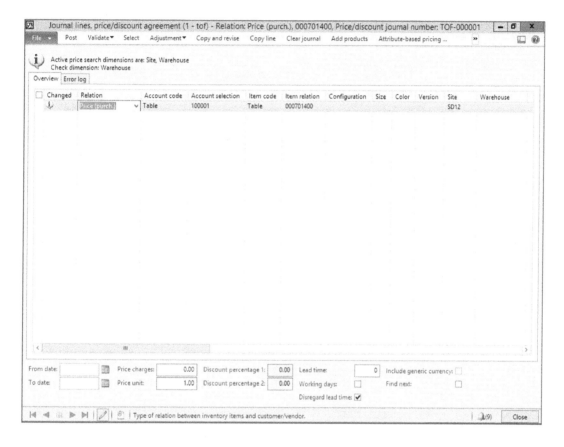

To do this, open up your **Trade Agreement Journal Lines** and click on the **Post** button in the menu bar.

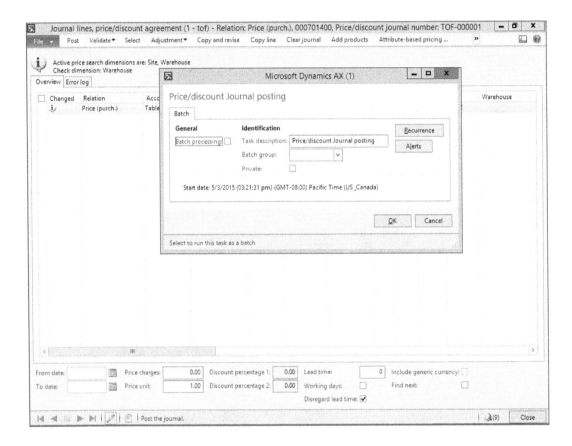

This will open up the **Price Discount Journal Posting** dialog box. All you need to do is click on the **OK** button.

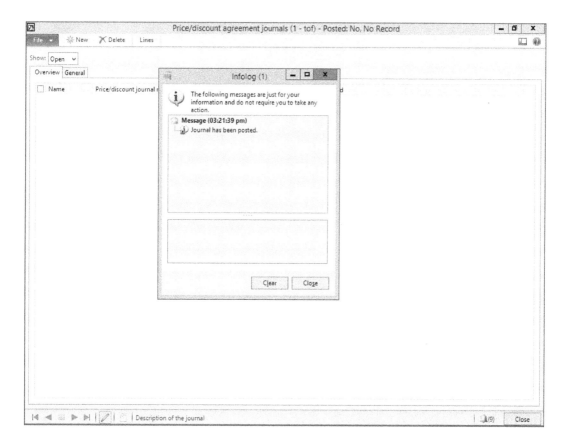

You will get a quick InfoLog that says that the Journal has been posted and you can just click the **Close** button to dismiss it.

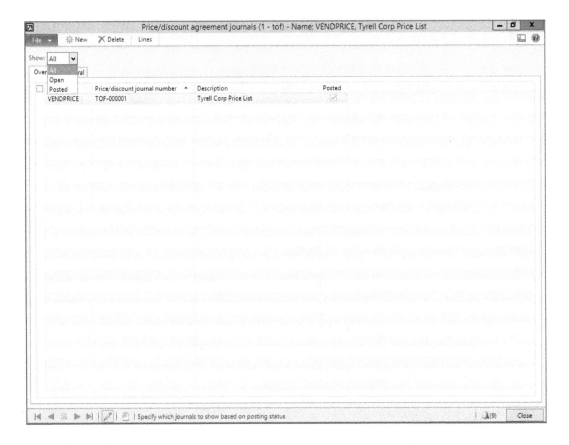

Once the **Price/Discount Agreement Journal** has been posted, you will notice that it disappears. That's because this form only shows the Open journals by default. If you click on the **Show** dropdown list and then select the **All** option you will see all of the posted journals as well.

Now that you are done, click on the **Close** button to exit from the form.

Using A Price List In A Purchase Order

Now that we have a **Vendor Price List** we can see it in action by creating a **Purchase Order**.

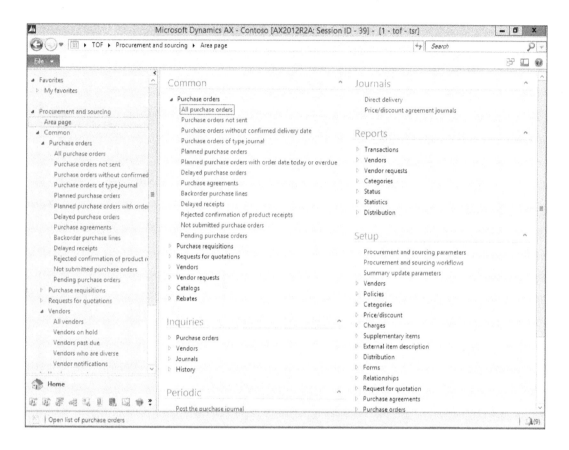

To do this, click on the **All Purchase Orders** menu item within the **Purchase Orders** folder of the **Common** group within the **Procurement and Sourcing** area page.

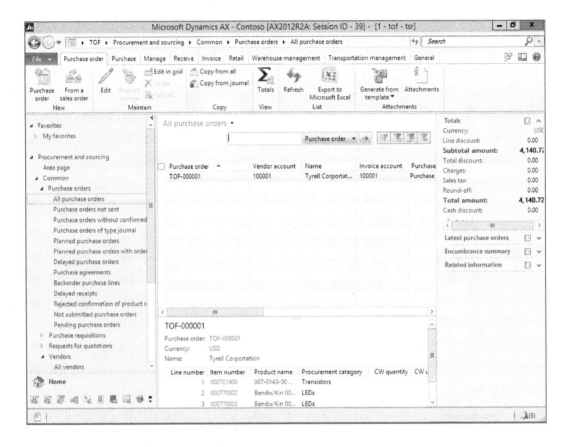

When the **All Purchase Orders** list page is displayed, click on the **Purchase Orders** button within the **New** group of the **Purchase Order** ribbon bar to create a new Purchase Order.

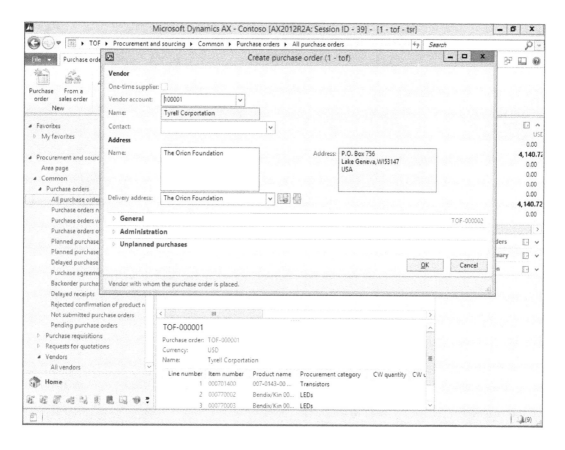

When the **Create Purchase Order** dialog box is displayed, type in the vendor that you created the Price List for (**100001**) and then click on the **OK** button.

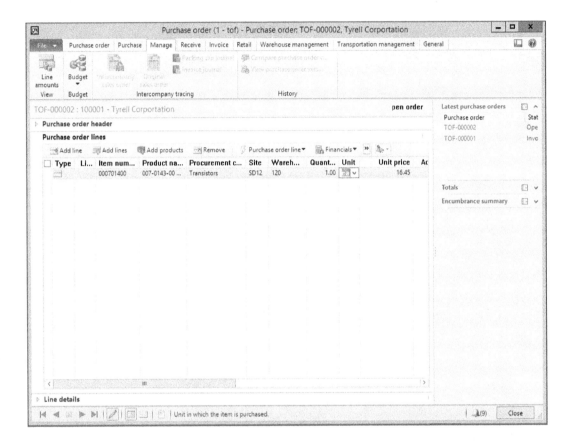

When the **Purchase Order Details** are displayed, enter in the **Item Number** that you assigned within the Price List (**000701400**) and you will see that the price now default in to be the price from the Trade Agreement and not the default on the Product.

Creating Price Lists From Categories

Since you have the **Procurement Categories** configured, then you can save even more time in setting up your price lists by adding lines to your price list by selecting then directly from the **Categories**. This definitely saves a lot of time as you are setting up larger price lists.

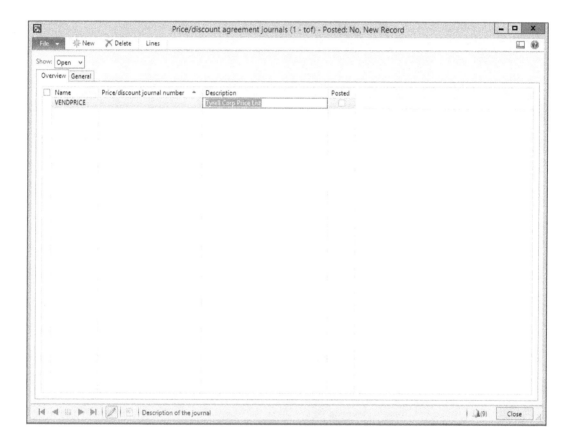

To do this, open up the **Price/Discount Agreement Journals**, click the **New** button to create a new record, set the Journal **Name** to **VENDPRICE** and the **Description** to **Tyrell Corp Price List**.

Then Click on the **Lines** button in the menu bar to go to the Journal Lines.

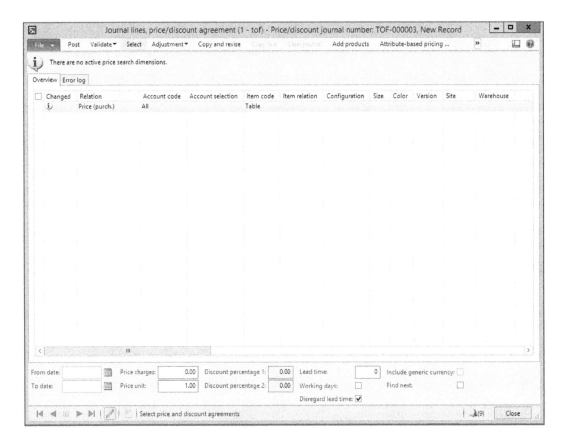

Now rather than entering in each of the products one-by-one, click on the **Add Products** button in the menu bar.

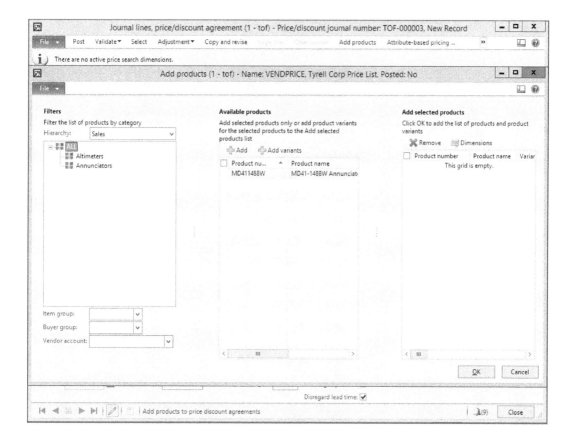

This will open up the **Add Products** form.

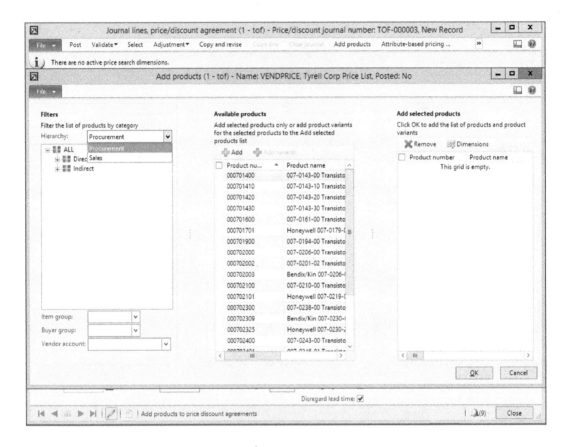

Click on the **Hierarchy** dropdown list and change the hierarchy from **Sales** to **Procurement** and you will see all of the products and hierarchies that you set up earlier on.

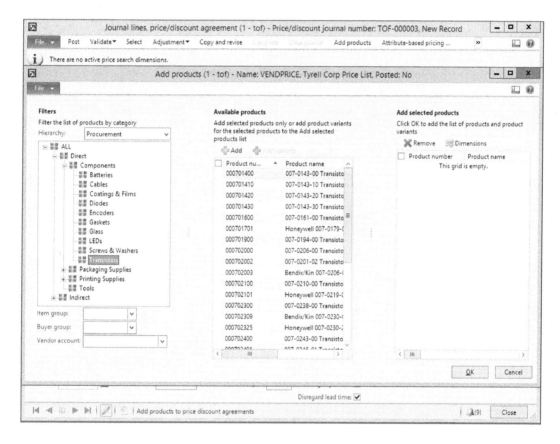

Drill into the categories down to the **Transistors** category and select it. You will see that only the **Transistors** are shown in the **Available Products** list.

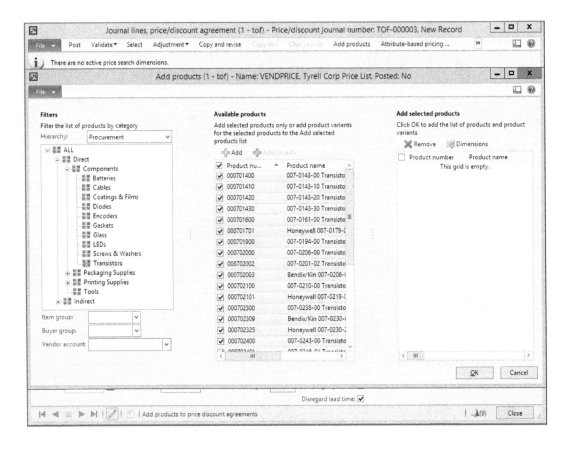

Select all of the products.

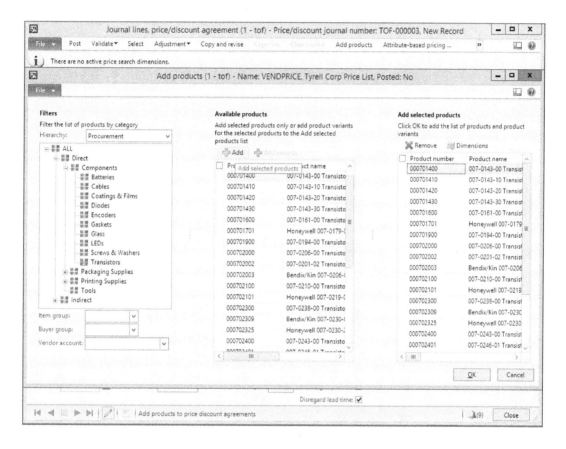

Then click on the **Add** button in the **Available Products** panel to add them to the **Add Selected Products** panel.

When you have done that, click on the **OK** button to add them to the Journal and to exit form the form.

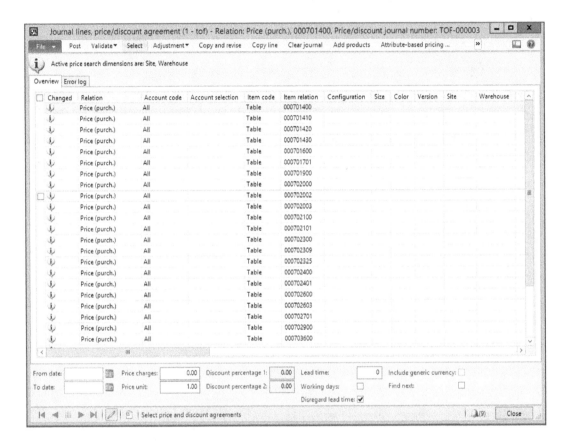

When you return to the **Journal Lines** you will see that all of the items have been added for you.

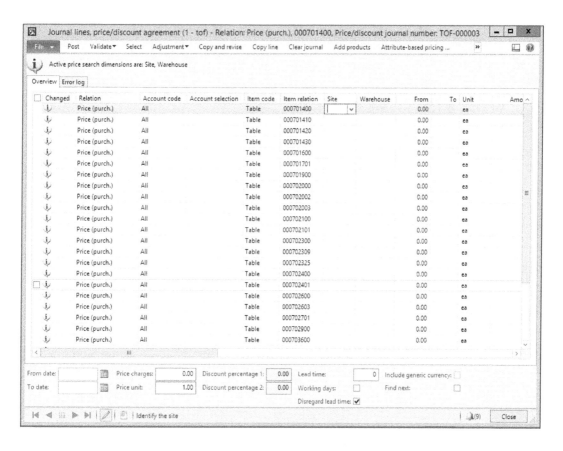

All you need to do is to polish the data and update the prices.

Updating The Pricing Using Excel

For larger journals you may want an easier way to maintain the prices, and most people want to do it within Excel. Luckily it just so happens that there is an option that allows you to do that.

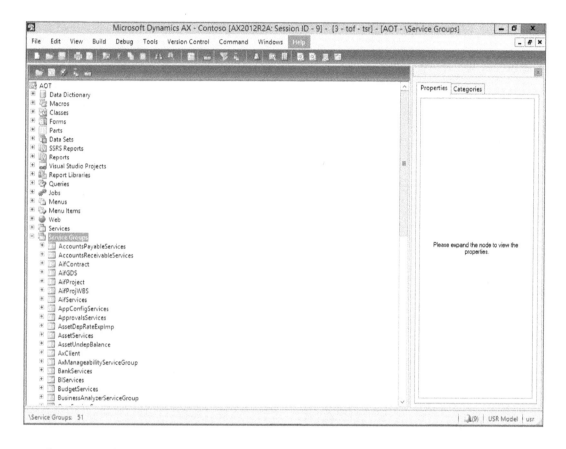

Before we can do this though we need to set up one thing and that is to deploy the service that will allow the prices to be updated from Excel. This may seem technical, but it's not really. To do this, open up the AOT development environment (just press **CTRL+D**) and expand out the **Service Groups** folder.

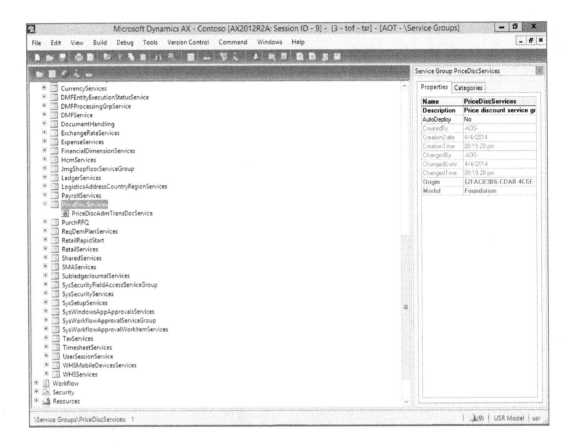

Then scroll down and find the **PriceDiscService**.

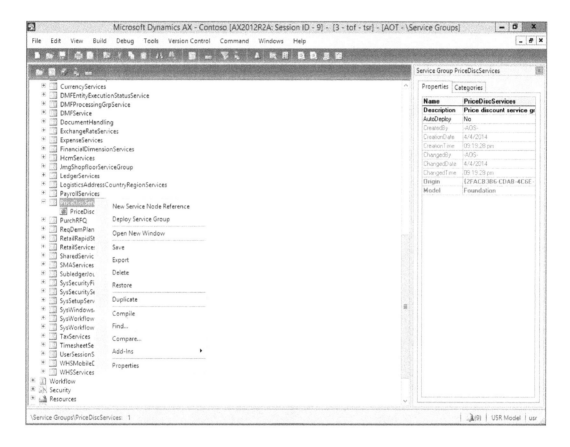

Right-mouse-click on the **PriceDiscService** and select the **Deploy Service Group** menu item.

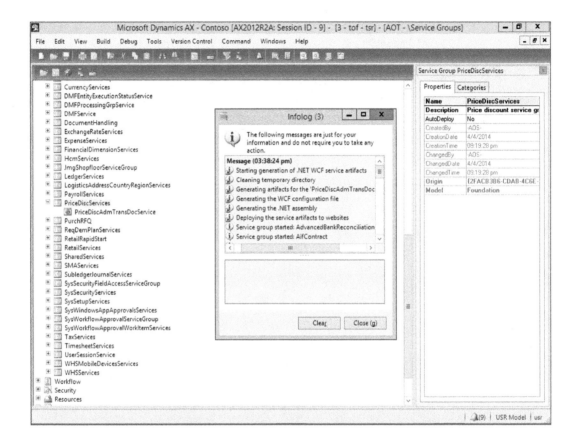

The system will run for a little bit, then you should get an InfoLog saying that the service was deployed. Click on the **Close** button to dismiss the message an then close out of **AOT** (press **ALT+F4**).

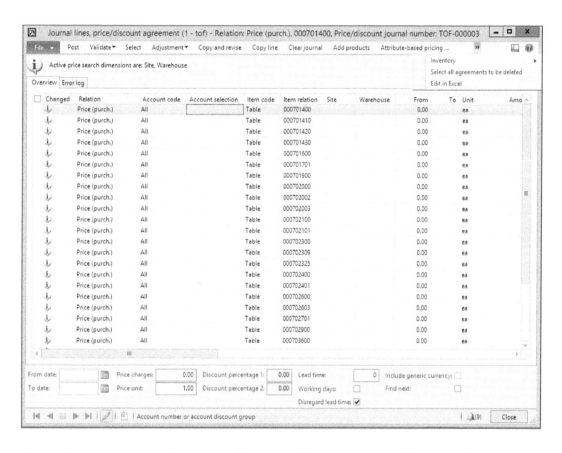

Now return to your Journal lines, and click on the **Edit In Excel** button in the menu bar.

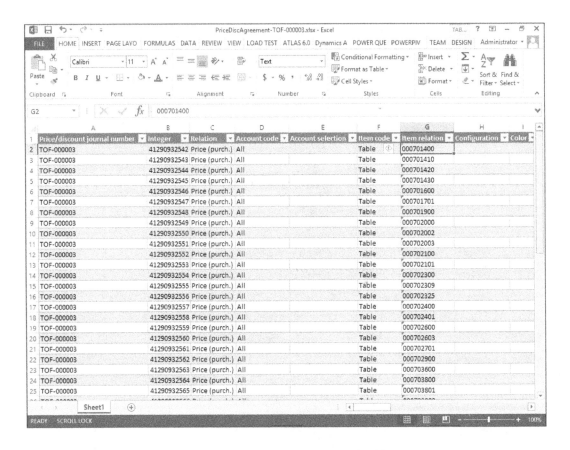

This will open up the **Trade Agreement Journal Lines** within Excel for you.

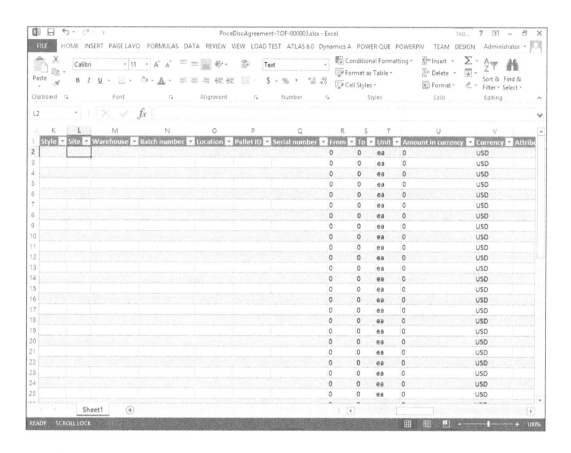

All of the fields from the Journal Lines area available for you including the **Site** and **Warehouse**.

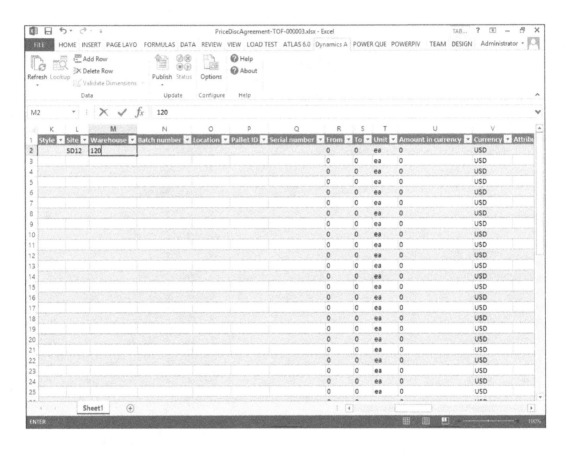

You can update an individual line...

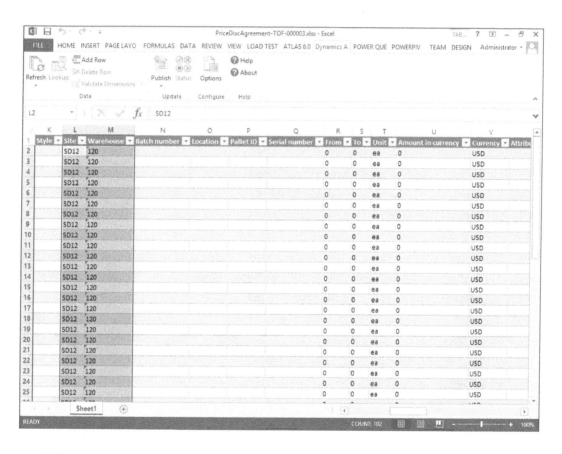

And then past the data into all of the other records by pressing **CTRL+D**.

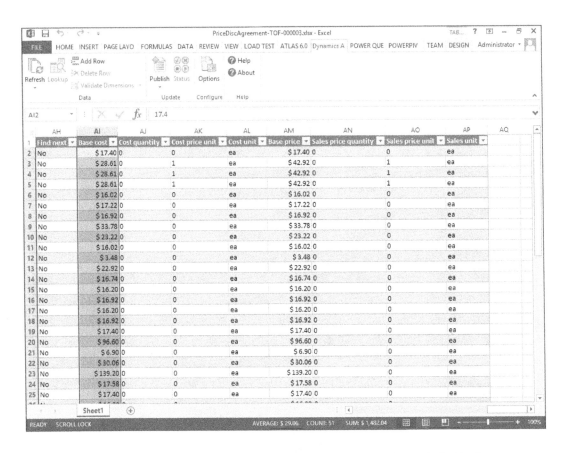

Also, if you scroll over to the right you will see that the **Base Cost** is also included in the worksheet showing all of the base costs from the products.

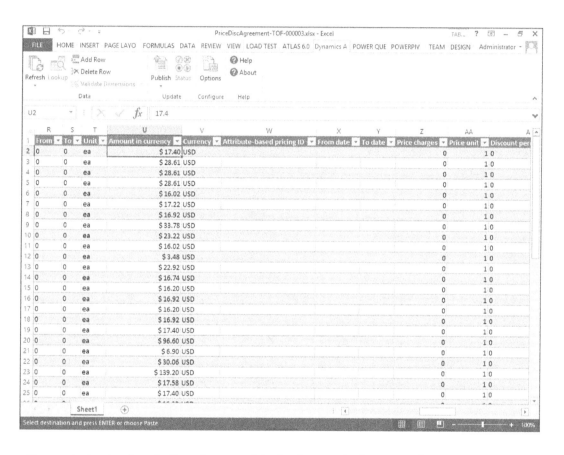

You can just cut and paste the values over into the **Amount in Currency** column.

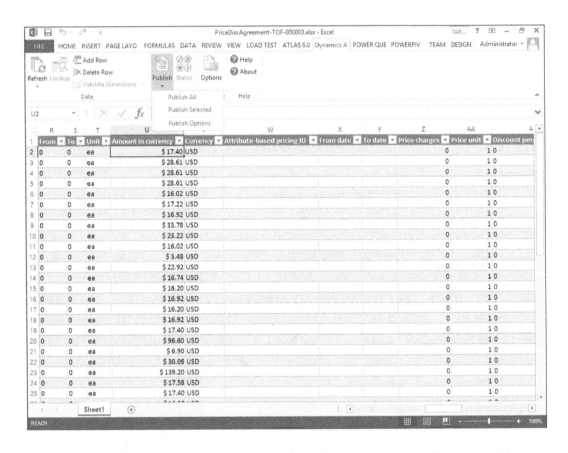

After updating all of the Journal Lines you can publish the data back to your Journal by clicking on the **Publish** button within the **Update** group of the **Dynamics AX** ribbon bar and select the **Publish All** menu item

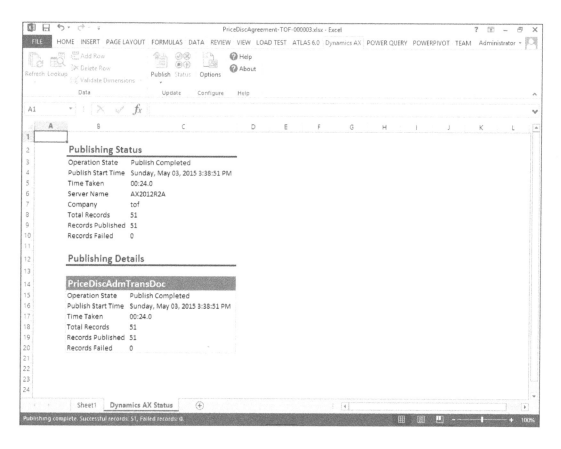

After it has updated all of the records, if you switch to the newly created **Dynamics AX Status** worksheet you will see a summary of the update and you can see how many records were updated.

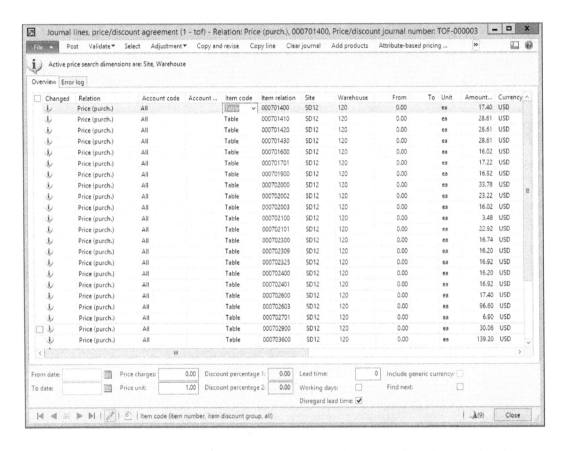

When you return to the **Journal Lines** you will see that all of the prices have been updated. Although we forgot to make this specific to the vendor.

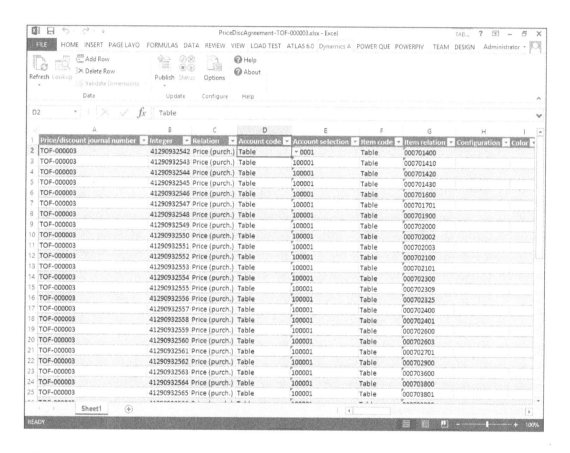

Don't worry, just return back to the worksheet and you can update the **Account Code** to be
Table and the **Account Selection** to be **100001**. Then click on the **Publish** button within the
Update group of the **Dynamics AX** ribbon bar again and select the **Publish All** menu item

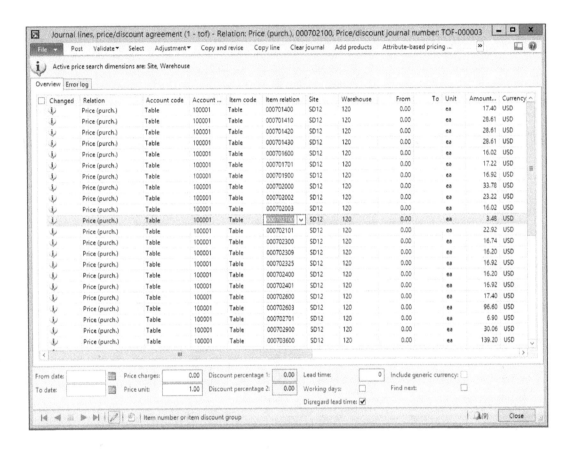

Now your price list has been refined to just the vendor.

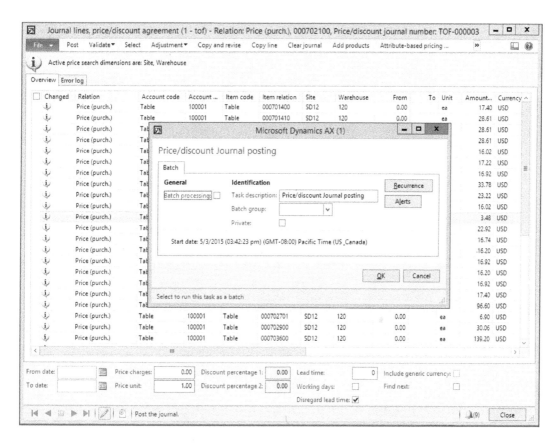

To finish the process, just click on the **Post** button in the menu bar, and when the
Price/Discount Journal Posting form is displayed, click on the **OK** button.

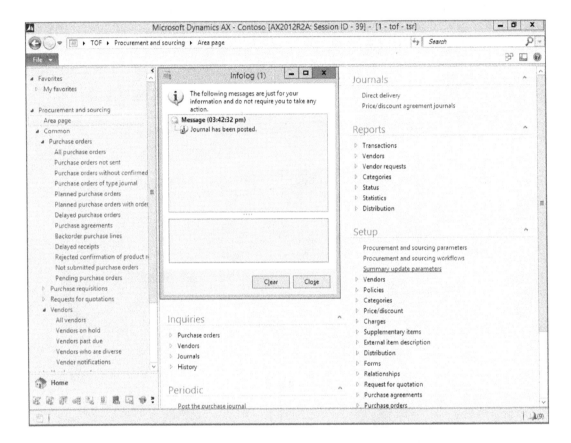

You will get an **Infolog** telling you that the Journal has been posted and you can dismiss the message by clicking on the **Close** button.

How easy is that?

Updating Sales Prices Directly From The Vendor Account

Once you have some **Trade Agreements** configured then you can take advantage of another feature which allows you to update the prices from the **Vendor** itself.

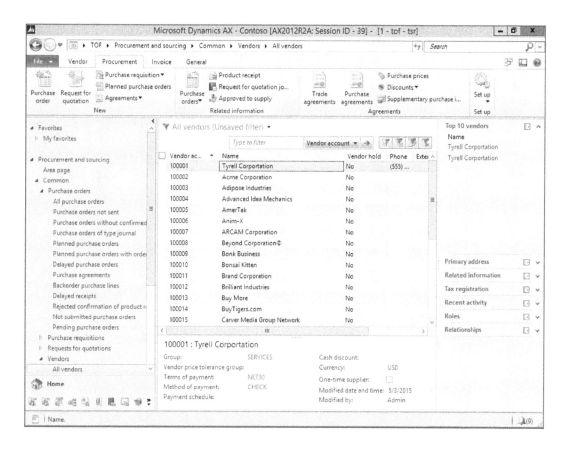

To do this, open up the **All Vendors** list page, select the **Vendor** record that you have created your Price Lists for (**100001**) and click on the **Trade Agreements** button within the **Agreements** group of the **Procurement** ribbon bar.

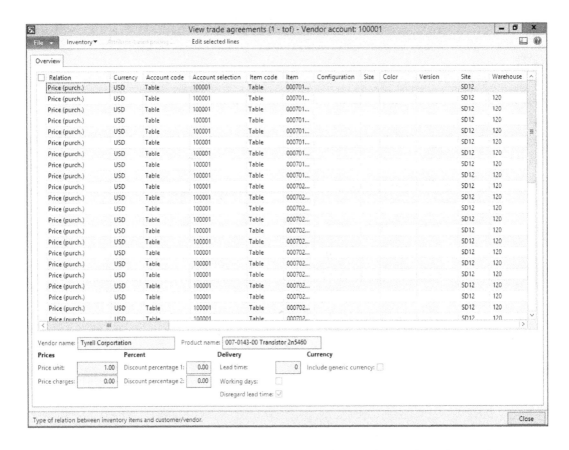

This will open up a list of all the **Trade Agreement Journal Lines** that apply to the Vendor.

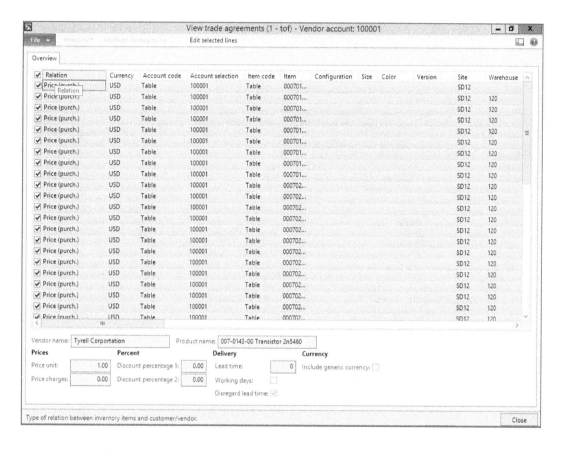

To update all of the agreement lines, click on the **Select All** checkbox in the top left of the grid and then click on the **Edit Selected Lines** button in the menu bar.

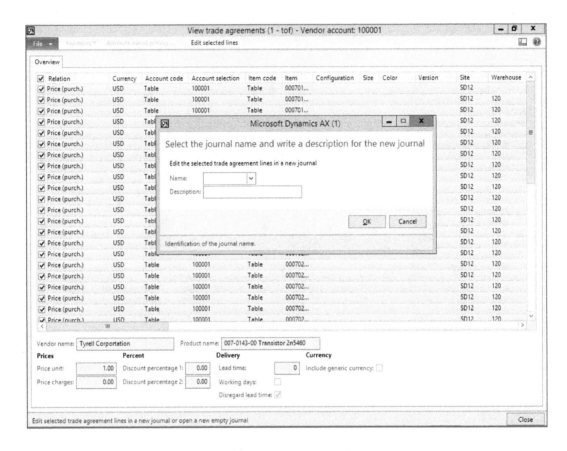

This will open up a new **Journal Name Selection** dialog box for you because we will be creating a new Trade Agreement through this process.

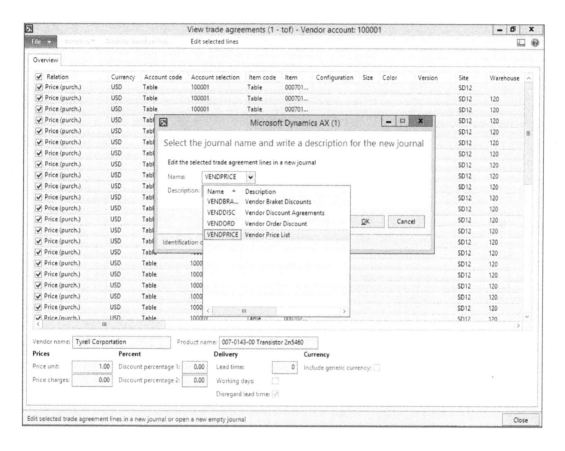

Click on the **Name** dropdown list and select the **VENDPRICE** code.

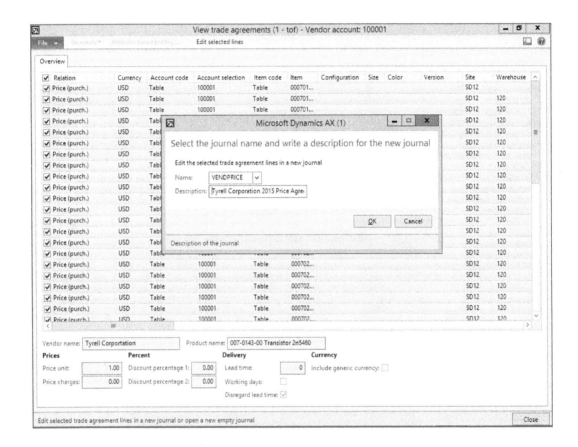

And then add a **Description**.

When you have done this, click on the **OK** button.

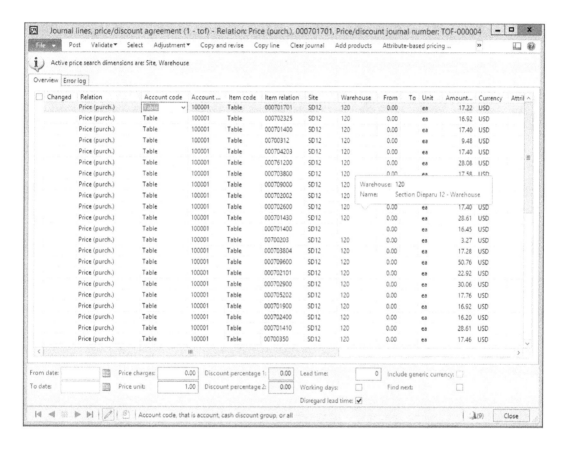

This will take you straight to the **Journal Lines** form with all of the lines that you selected automatically populated.

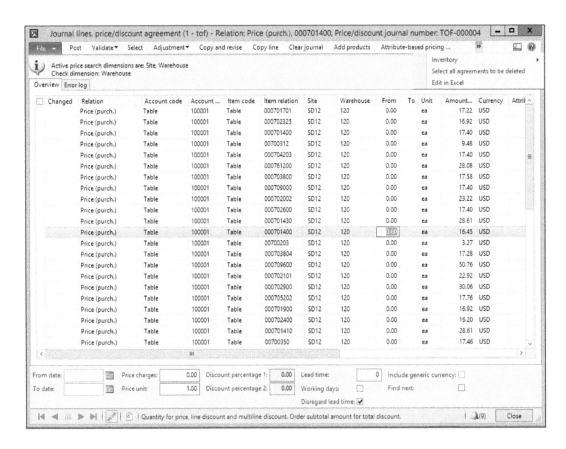

Now click on the **Edit In Excel** button in the menu bar.

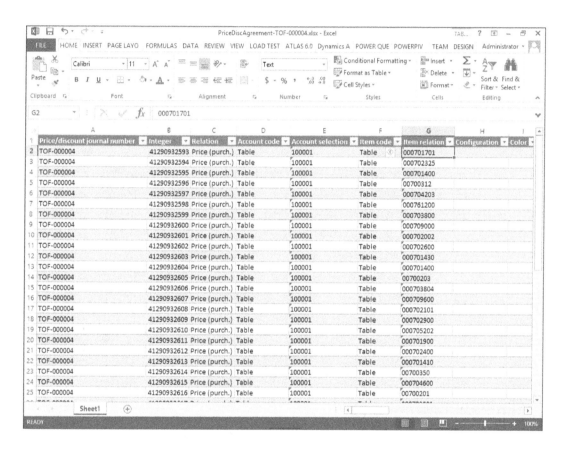

This will open up Excel with all of the lines from the **Trade Agreement Journal**.

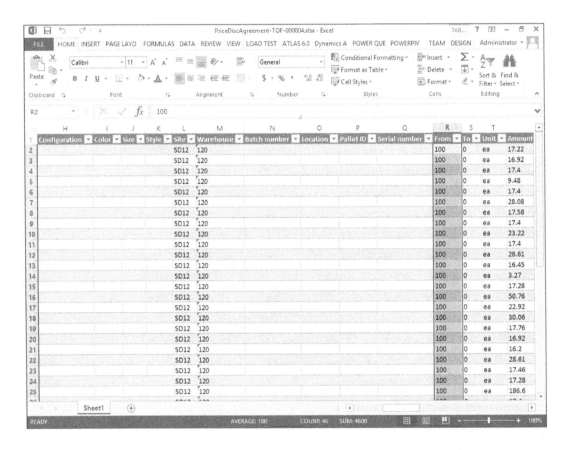

Configuration	Color	Size	Style	Site	Warehouse	Batch number	Location	Pallet ID	Serial number	From	To	Unit	Amount
				SD12	120					100	0	ea	17.22
				SD12	120					100	0	ea	16.92
				SD12	120					100	0	ea	17.4
				SD12	120					100	0	ea	9.48
				SD12	120					100	0	ea	17.4
				SD12	120					100	0	ea	28.08
				SD12	120					100	0	ea	17.58
				SD12	120					100	0	ea	17.4
				SD12	120					100	0	ea	23.22
				SD12	120					100	0	ea	17.4
				SD12	120					100	0	ea	28.61
				SD12	120					100	0	ea	16.45
				SD12	120					100	0	ea	3.27
				SD12	120					100	0	ea	17.28
				SD12	120					100	0	ea	50.76
				SD12	120					100	0	ea	22.92
				SD12	120					100	0	ea	30.06
				SD12	120					100	0	ea	17.76
				SD12	120					100	0	ea	16.92
				SD12	120					100	0	ea	16.2
				SD12	120					100	0	ea	28.61
				SD12	120					100	0	ea	17.46
				SD12	120					100	0	ea	17.28
				SD12	120					100	0	ea	186.6

We are going to change this agreement slightly by specifying a **From** quantity of **100** and pasting it into all of the lines. This is going to say that the price that we specify here is only valid for orders of over 100 units.

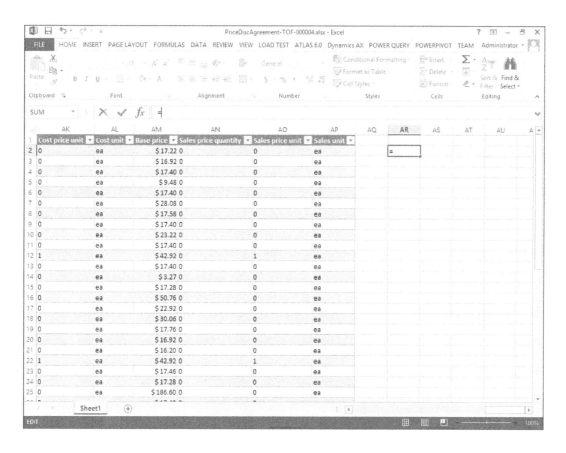

The other benefit of Excel is that we can use formulas and calculations which is what we will do here. To the right of the table (not directly adjacent) start a formula by typing =.

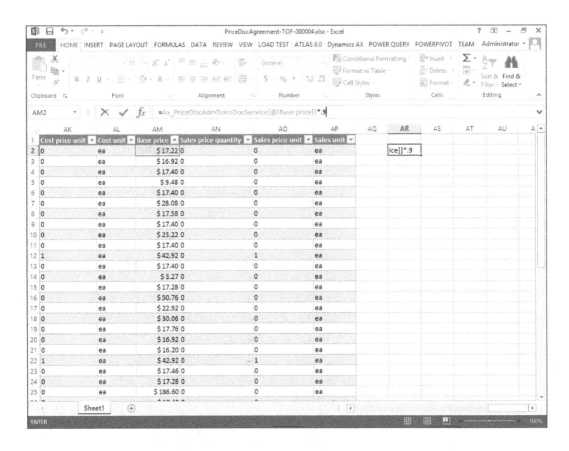

Then select the **Base Price** cell and then type in ***.9** to create a 10% discounted price.

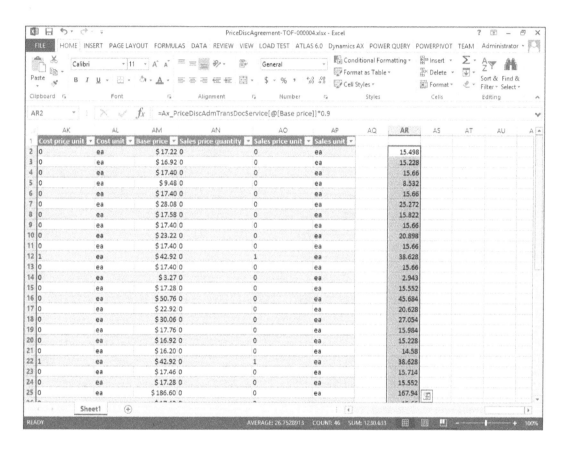

And then fill down to the end of the table.

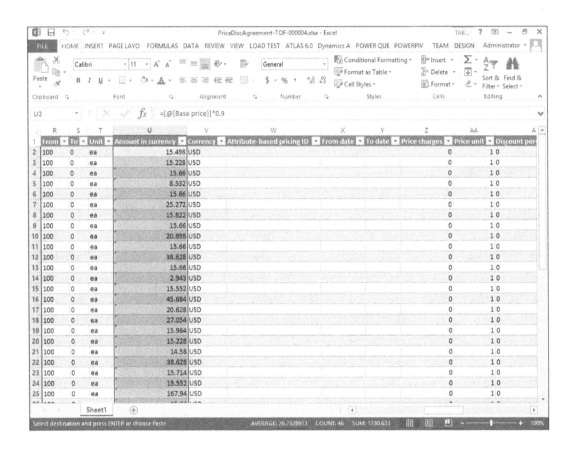

Now you can copy those values and pate them into the **Amount In Currency** column.

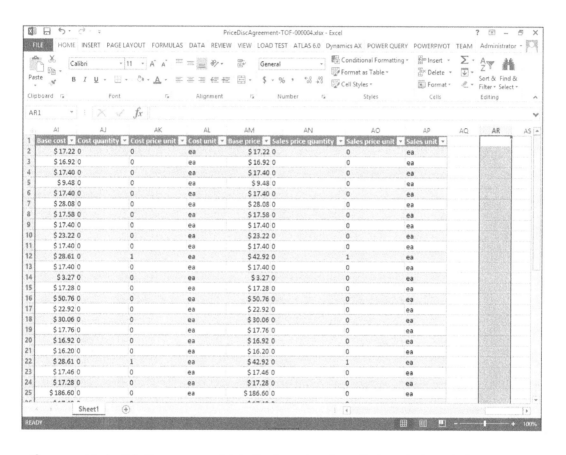

If you want to be tidy then you can delete the formula column that you just created.

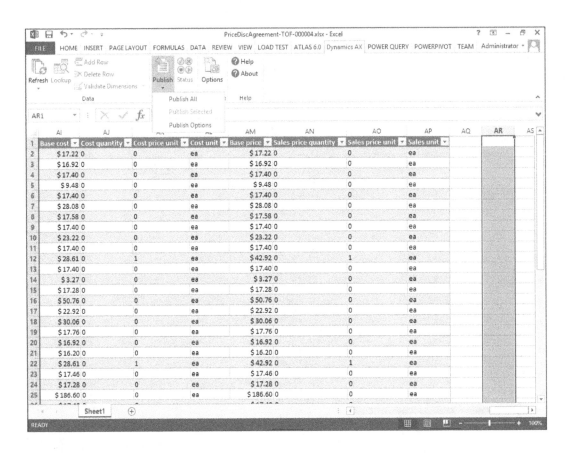

Now publish the data back to your Journal by clicking on the **Publish** button within the **Update** group of the **Dynamics AX** ribbon bar and select the **Publish All** menu item

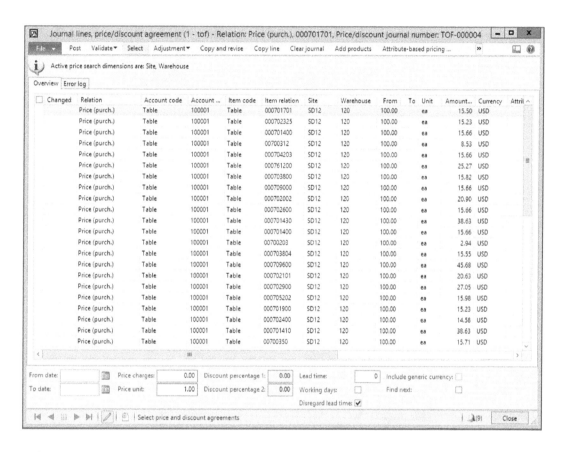

Now when you return to the **Journal Lines** you will see that the **From** quantity has updated and also the **Amount In Currency** has been adjusted.

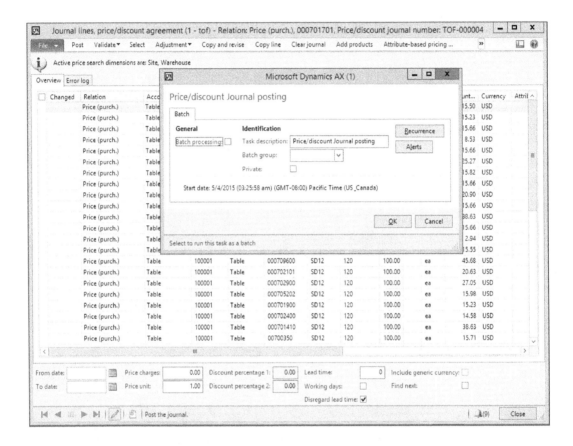

To finish off the process, just click on the **Post** button within the menu bar, and when the
Price/Discount Journal Posting dialog box is displayed, click on the **OK** button to post the
Journal.

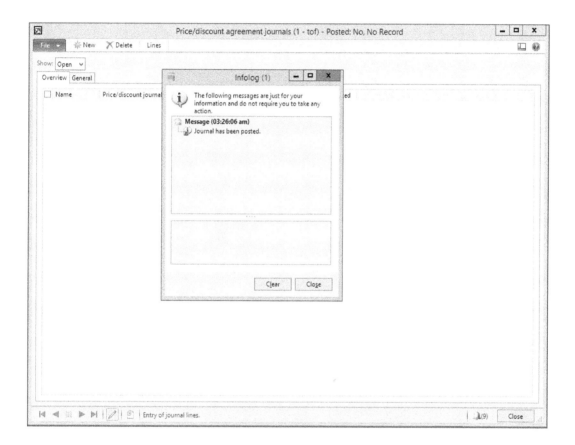

When the InfoLog is displayed, just click on the **Close** button to dismiss it and then click on the **Close** button to exit from the **Price/Discount Agreement Journals** form.

That will return you back to the **All Vendors** list page.

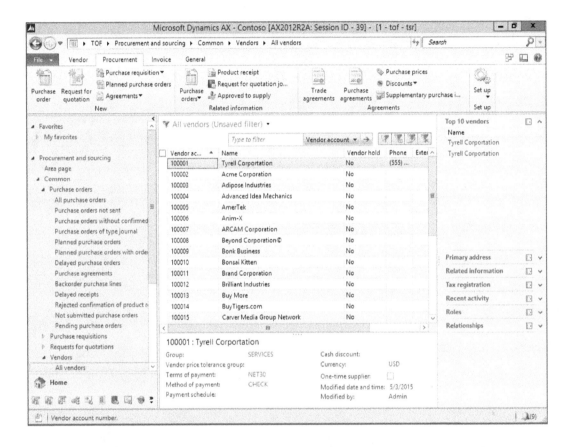

We can test this our directly from here by creating a PO for the Vendor. To do that just click on the **Purchase Order** button within the **New** group of the **Procurement** ribbon bar.

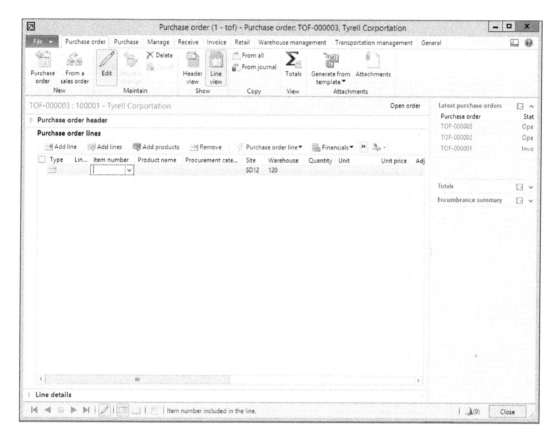

This will bypass the vendor selection dialog because it already knew the vendor that you had selected and take you straight into the **Purchase Order Details**.

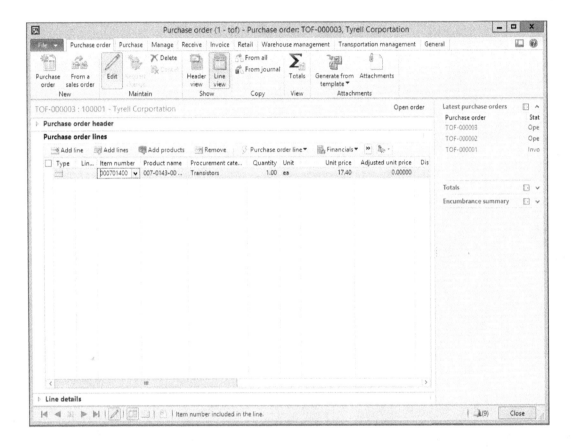

This time, if you enter in a Purchase Line for the product we used before, then the default price is displayed.

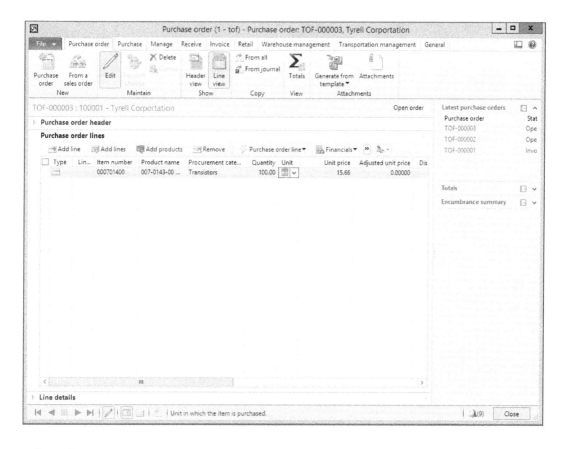

If you change the quantity to **100** then the price changes to the amount from the **Trade Agreement Journal**.

Creating A Discount Agreement For A Vendor

In addition to creating **Price Lists** you can also create **Discount Agreements** attached to your vendors that allow you to automatically apply discounts to your Purchase Orders.

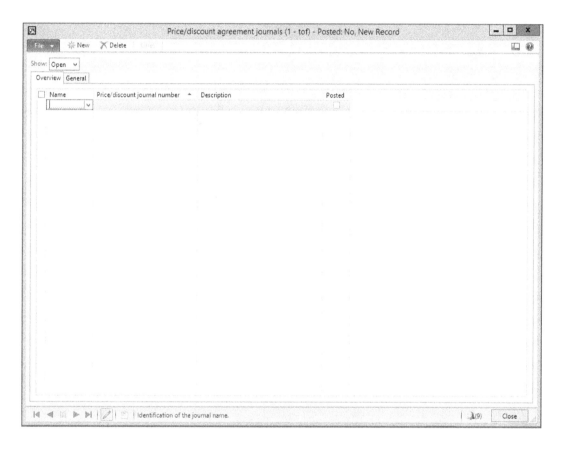

To do this, open up your **Price/Discount Agreement Journals** list page and click the **New** button to create a new record.

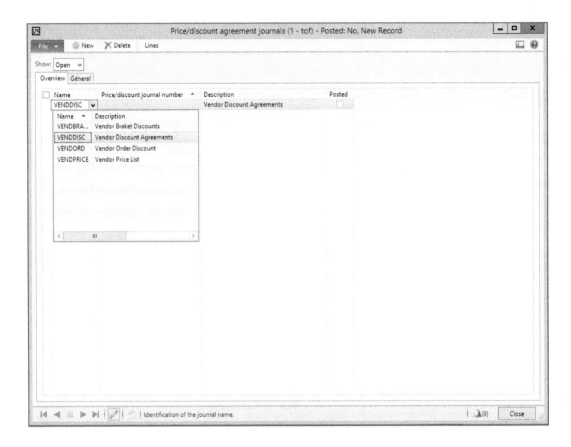

Then click on the **Name** dropdown list and select the **VENDDISC** Journal Name.

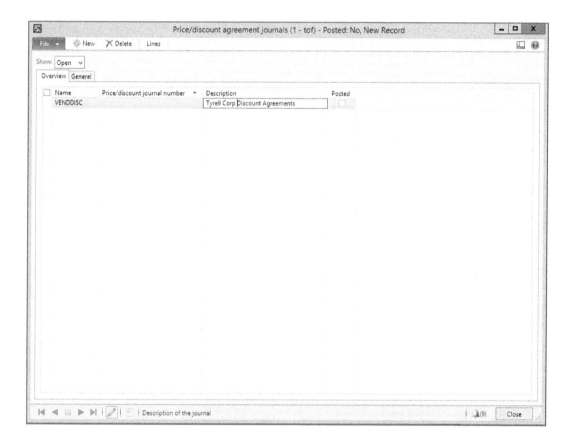

Then update the **Description** to make it a little more descriptive.

After you have done that, click on the **Lines** button in the menu bar.

When the **Journal Lines** will already be populated with a line, except this time the **Relation** will be **Line disc. (Purch)** which defaulted in from the Journal Name.

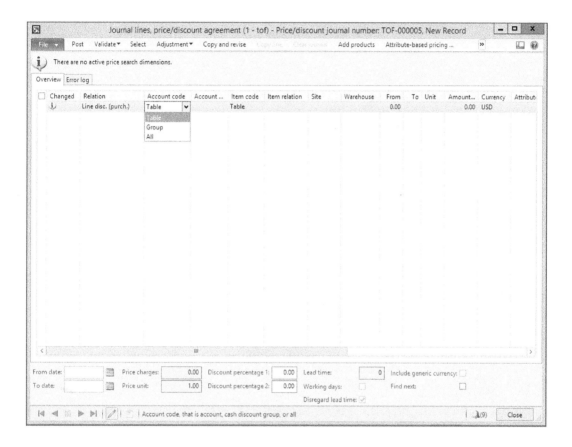

Click on the **Account Code** dropdown and select the **Table** value.

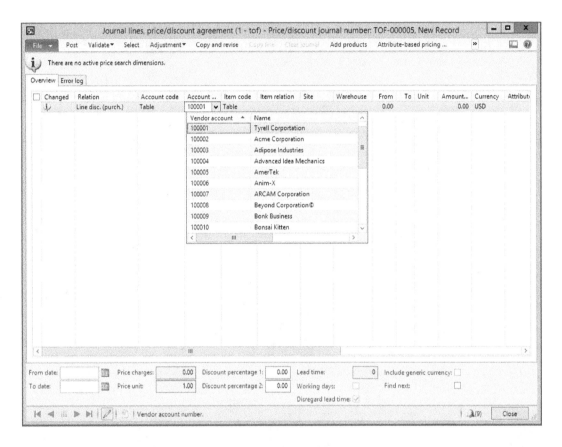

And then click on the **Account** dropdown list and select the **Vendor** that you want to receive the discount from. In this case we will choose **100001**.

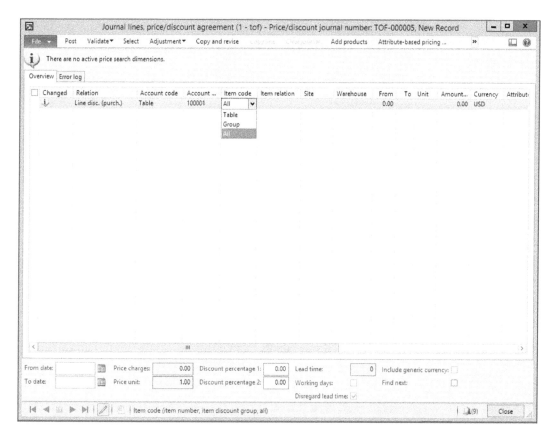

Next click on the **Item Code** dropdown list and change the value to **All** which will mean that the line discount will apply to all products purchased from them.

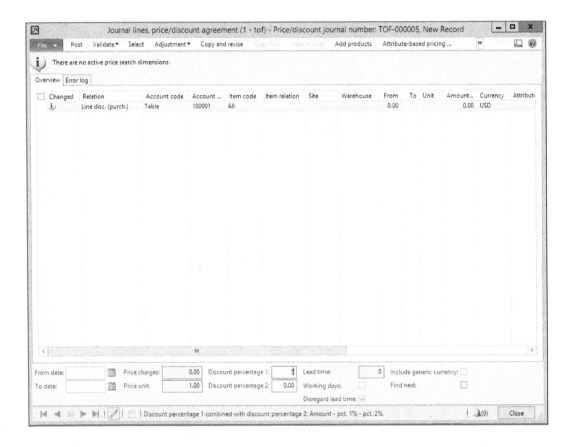

Now down in the footer, set the **Discount Percentage 1** to be **5** to indicate that this line has a 5% discount.

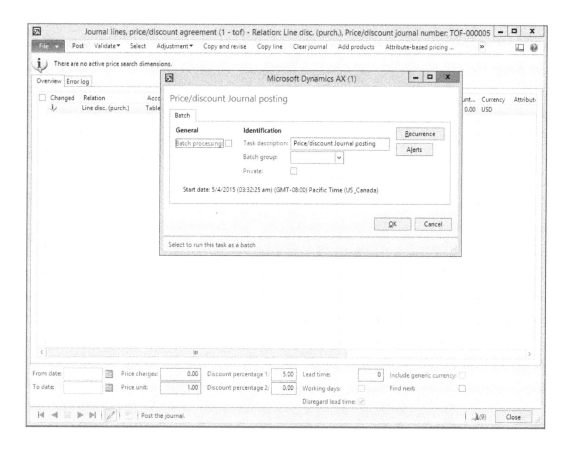

Now click on the **Post** button in the menu bar, and when the **Price/Discount Journal Posting** dialog is displayed, click on the **OK** button.

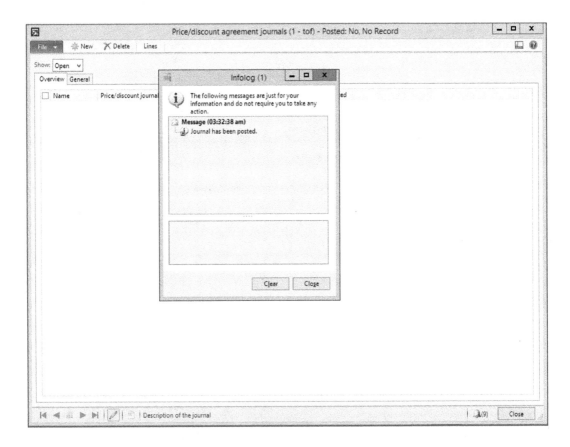

You will receive a confirmation **InfoLog** which you can click the **Close** button to dismiss.

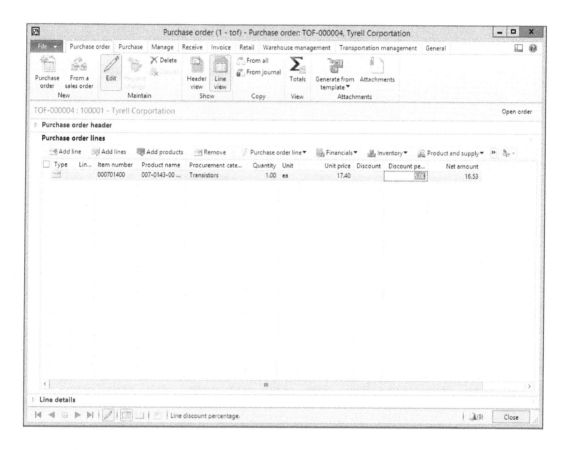

To test this out, create a new Purchase Order for the vendor that you created the agreements for (10001) and for the item that you have the price agreement for **(000701400)** and you will notice that there is now a discount applied to the Purchase Order Line.

How cool is that?

Viewing The Trade Agreements On Purchase Orders

If you want you can view all of the possible trade agreements for the line directly from the Purchase Order itself. This is a great way to validate that the pricing is working correctly.

To do this, open up your **Purchase Order** and then click on the **Purchase Order Line** button in the Line menu bar and select the **Price Details** submenu item.

Note: This is only visible if you enable it within the Procurement and Sourcing Parameters – which we did right at the start if this book.

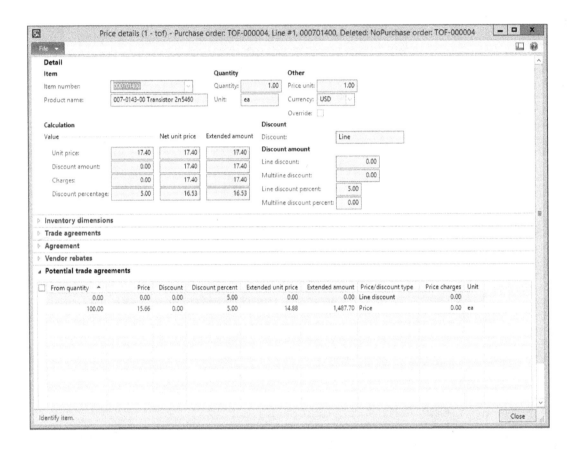

This will open up the **Price Details** form and if you expand out the **Potential Trade Agreements** tab then you will see the different prices and discount combinations that are eligible against this line.

Very cool.

ENABLING CHANGE MANAGEMENT ON PURCHASE ORDERS

If you want to track your Purchase Orders a little more closely, then you can turn on the **Change Management** feature within the Procurement and Sourcing module which gives you the added ability to have workflow approvals on your Purchase Orders. As a bonus this will also give you the ability to view the old versions of the Purchase Orders and see the differences between them.

In this chapter we will show how you can configure the change management feature and also build the workflows to manage the approval process.

Creating An Order Change Approval Workflow

Before we turn on the Purchase Order Change Management we need to create a workflow that will be used to manage the Purchase Order approval process.

Enable Change Management On Purchase Orders To Track Changes

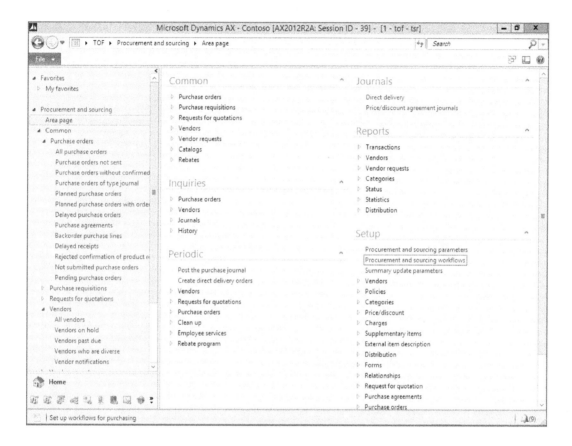

To do this, click on the **Procurement and Sourcing Workflows** menu item within the **Setup** group of the **Procurement and Sourcing** area page.

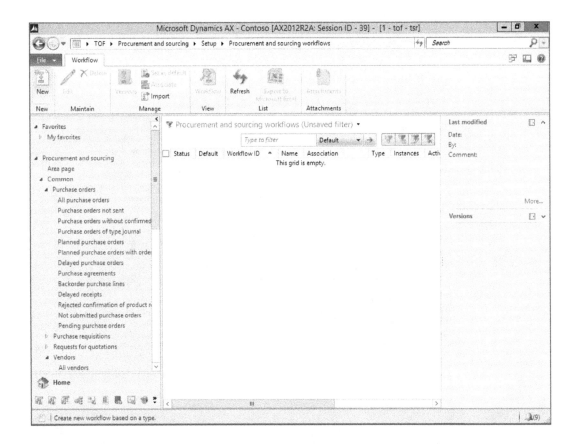

When the **Procurement and Sourcing** list page is displayed, click on the **New** button within the **New** group of the **Workflow** ribbon bar.

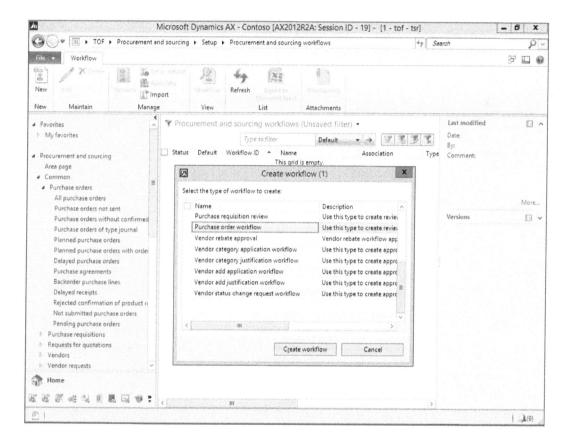

When the **Create Workflow** dialog box is displayed, select the **Purchase Order Workflow** option and click on the **Create Workflow** button.

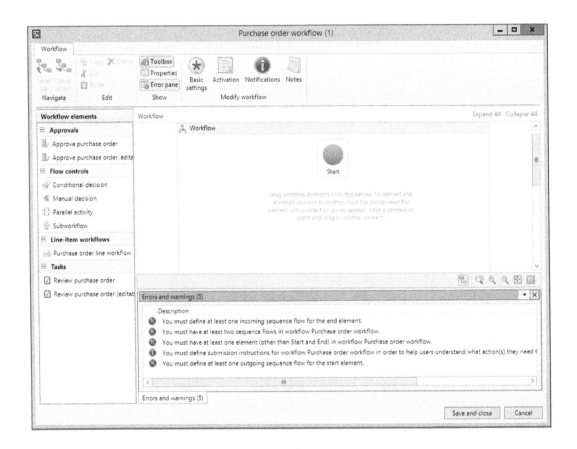

This will open up the workflow designer canvas.

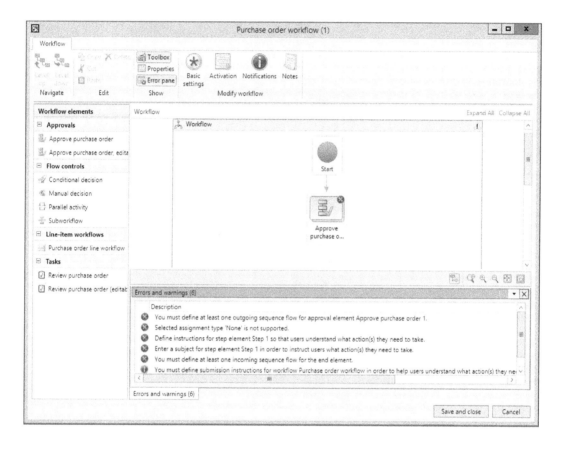

Drag the **Approve Purchase Order** workflow element from the palette on the left onto the canvas and link it with the **Start** element.

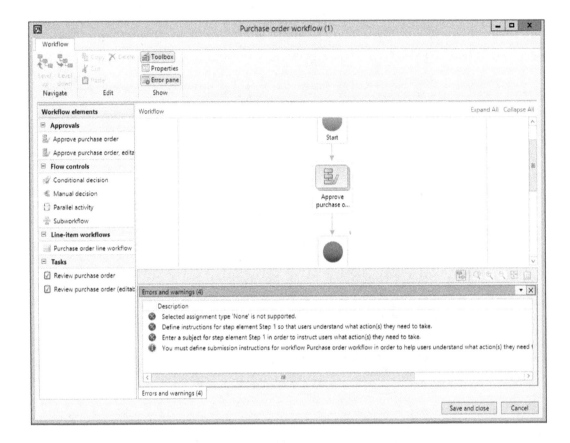

Then link the **Approve Purchase Order** element with the **Finish** element to create a complete workflow.

Now double click on the first error message which is indicating that a User has not been assigned to the workflow step.

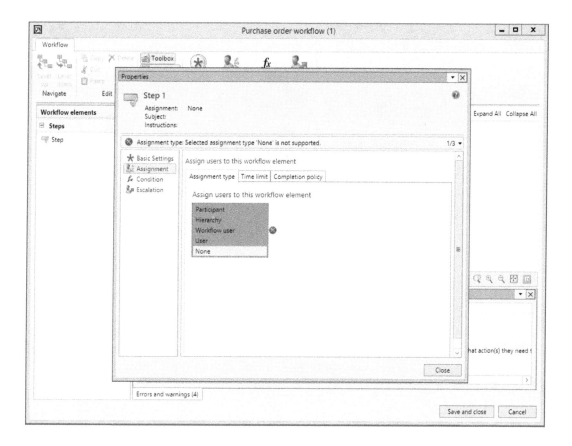

That will take you into the workflow element properties and to the **Assignment** page.

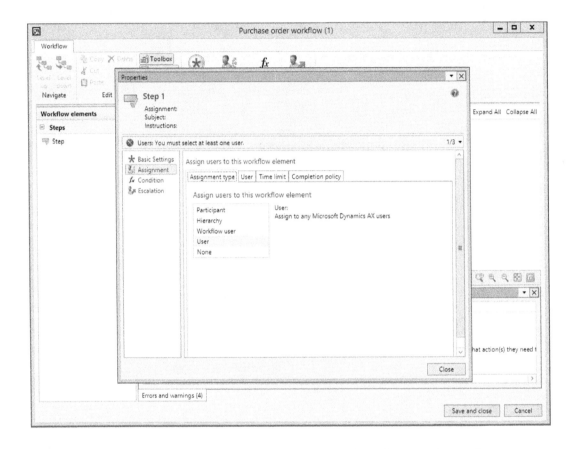

Select the **User** option within the **Assign Users to this Workflow Element** selection box.

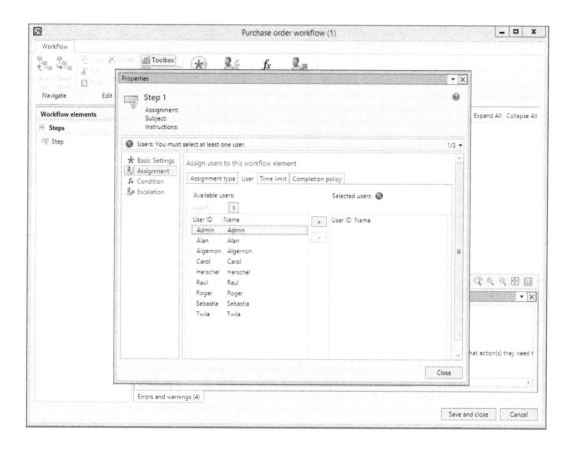

Now switch to the **Users** tab and you will see all of the system users.

Select the **Admin** user and click on the **>** button.

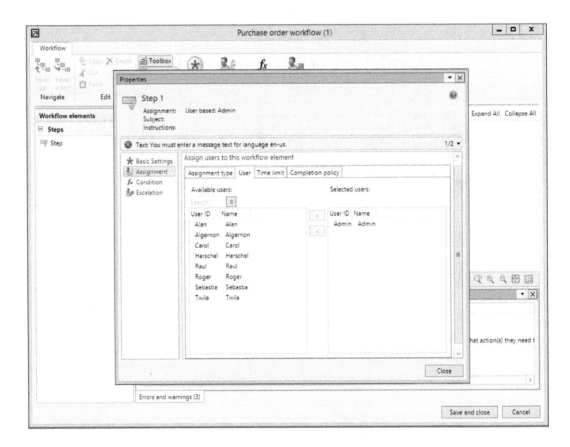

This will add it to the **Selected Users** list. Now click on the **Close** button to exit from the dialog box.

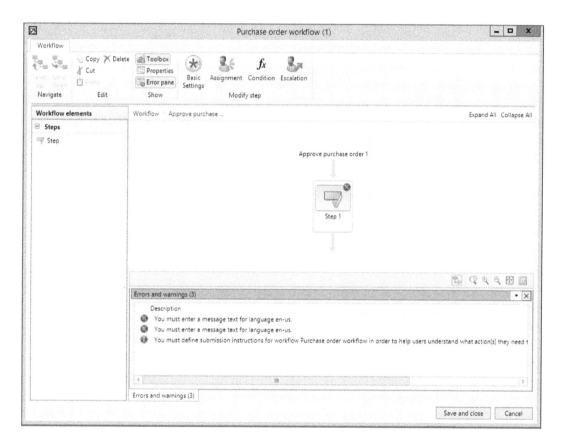

Now click on the next error message which is telling you that you need to add some message details on the workflow task.

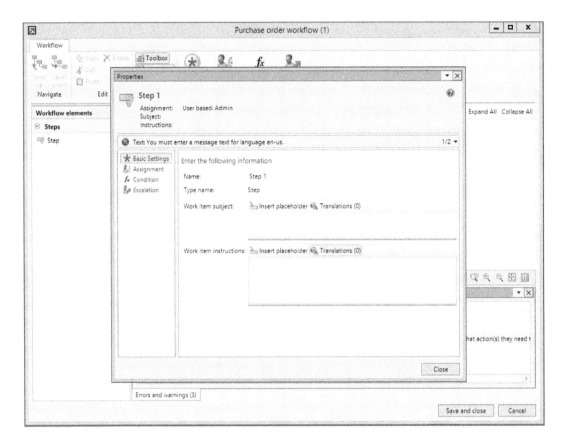

This will open up the **Basic Settings** page for the workflow element and you will see with the red squiggles that you need to add some text.

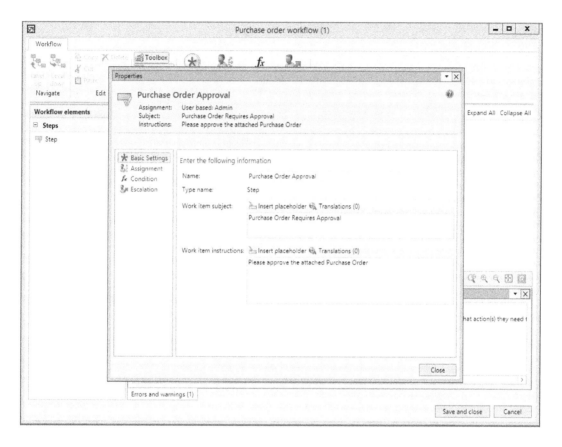

Type into the **Work Item Subject** a quick summary of the task that is being assigned to the user. For example: **Purchase Order Requires Approval**.

And then type into the **Work Item Instructions** a more detailed explanation of the task that is being assigned to the user. For example: **Please approve the attached Purchase Order**.

When you are done, click on the **Close** button to exit from the dialog box.

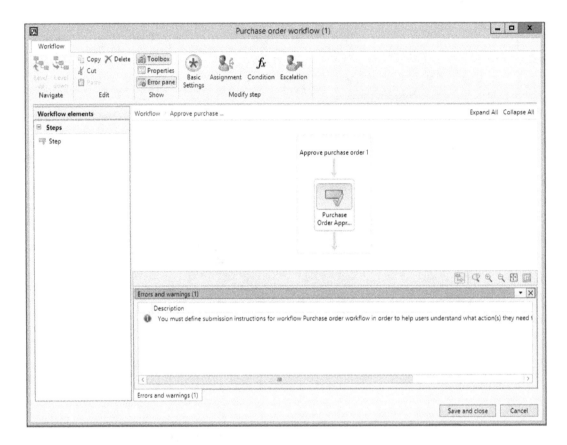

Now double click on the final warning message that is displayed in the **Errors and Warnings** panel.

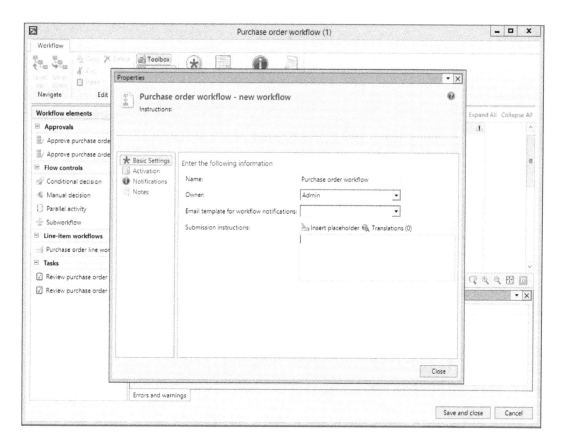

This will open up the **Basic Settings** for the workflow itself where you will want to configure the Submission details.

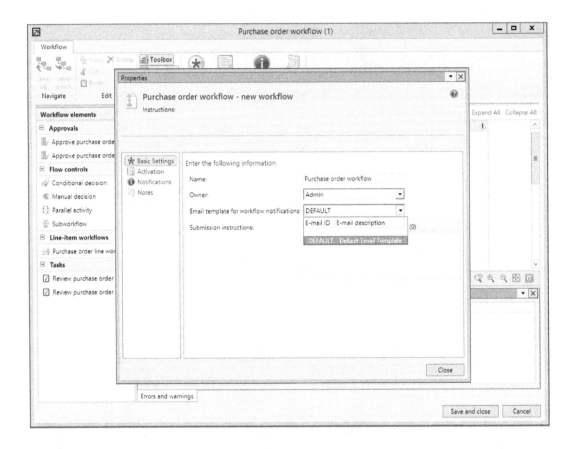

First, click on the **Email Template for Workflow Instructions** dropdown list and select the
DEFAULT e-mail template.

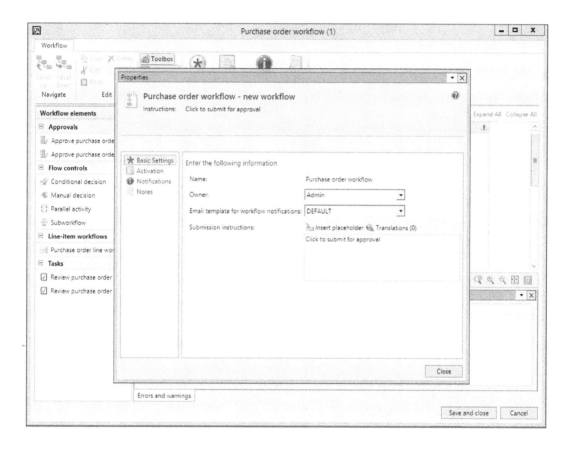

Then type in you **Submission Instructions** which will accompany the workflow and give the user more information as to what they are doing when they click on the **Submit** button. For Example: **Click to submit for approval**.

After you have done that, click on the **Close** button to exit from the form.

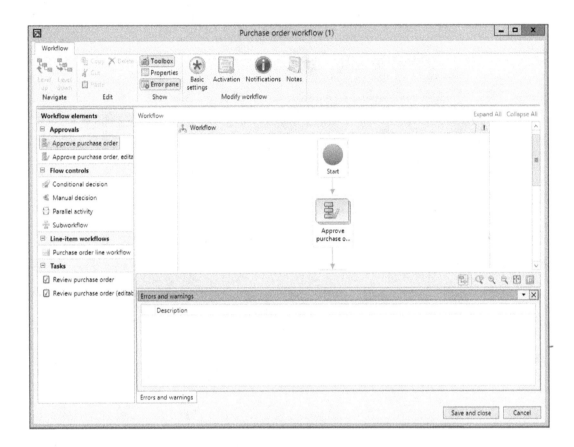

Now that you don't have any errors or warnings click on the **Save and Close** button.

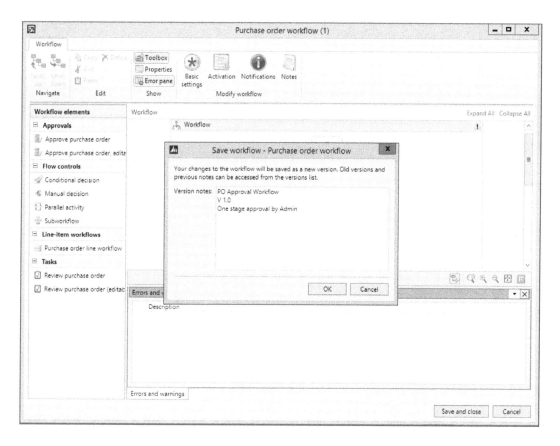

When the **Save Workflow** dialog is displayed, you can type in any **Version Notes** that you may want to describe this workflow, and then click on the **OK** button to save the workflow.

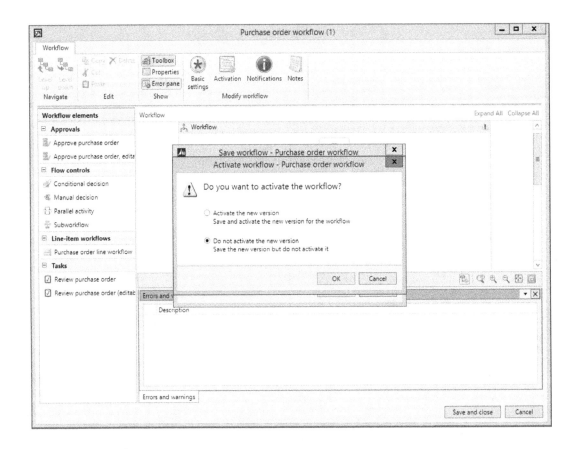

Then you will be asked if you want to **Activate** the workflow.

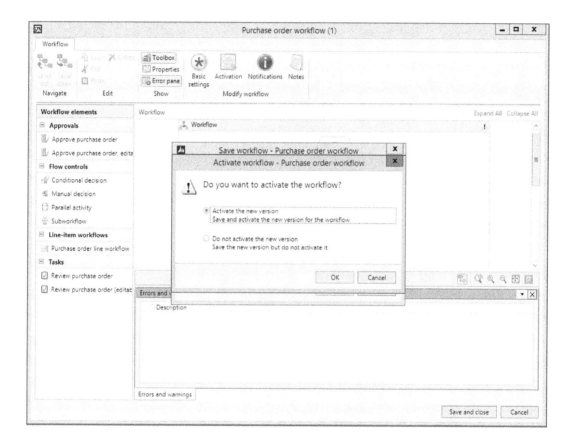

Select the **Activate the new version** radio button and then click on the **OK** button.

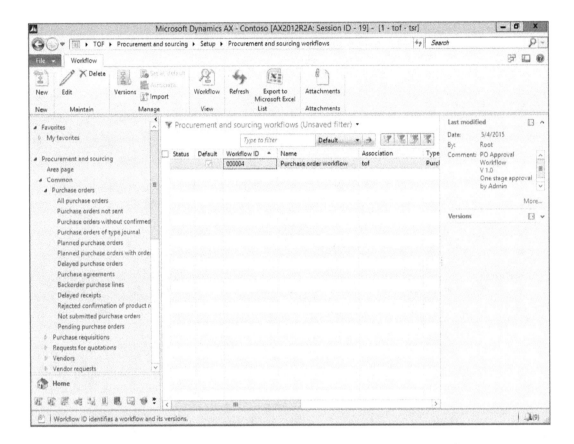

That will return you back to the **Procurement and Sourcing Workflows** list page and you will see that you have a new workflow.

That was easy.

Enabling Purchase Order Change Management

Now that we have a workflow, we will want to enable **Change Management** on our **Purchase Orders**.

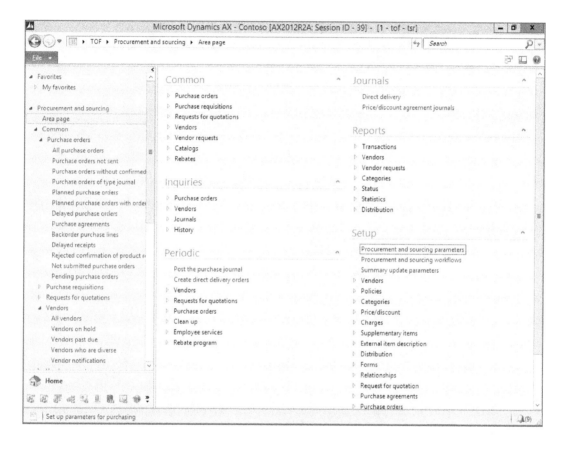

To do this click on the **Procurement and Sourcing Parameters** menu item within the **Setup** group of the **Procurement and Sourcing** area page.

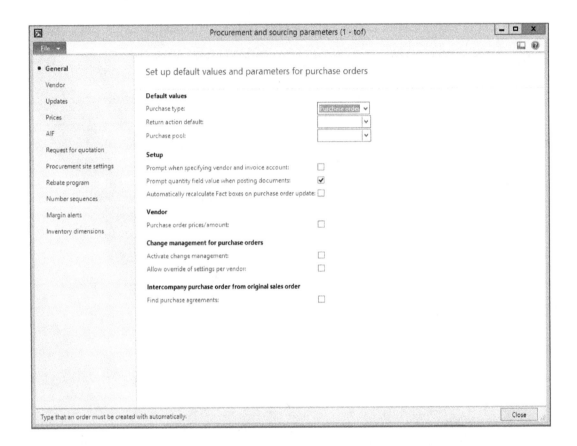

When the **Procurement and Sourcing Parameters** maintenance form is displayed, make sure that you are on the **General** page.

Enable Change Management On Purchase Orders To Track Changes

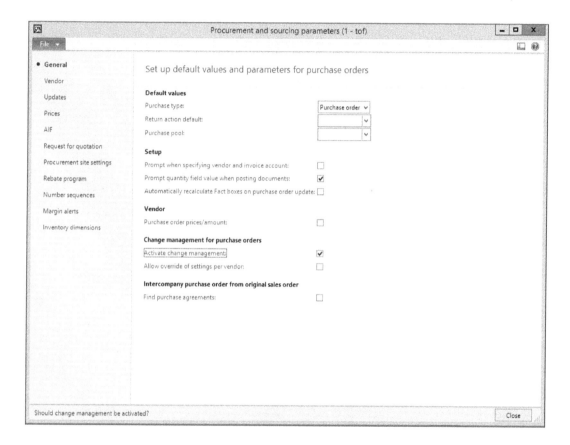

All you need to do is check the **Activate Change Management** flag within the **Change Management For Purchase Orders** group.

After you have done that, click on the **Close** button to exit from the form.

Enable Change Management On Purchase Orders To Track Changes

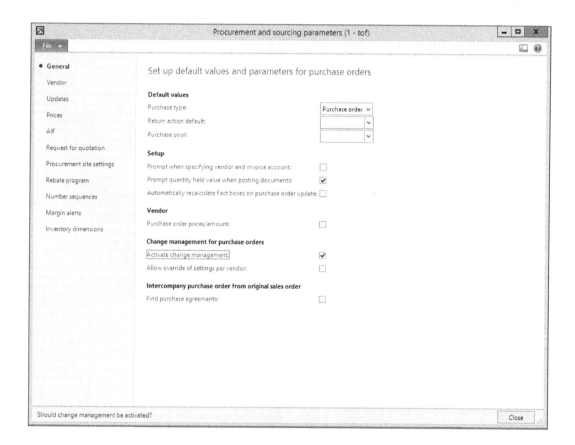

All you need to do is check the **Activate Change Management** flag within the **Change Management For Purchase Orders** group.

After you have done that, click on the **Close** button to exit from the form.

Submitting A PO For Approval

Now that you have configured the **Change Management** workflow and turned on the feature, we can start using it within our **Purchase Orders**.

Enable Change Management On Purchase Orders To Track Changes

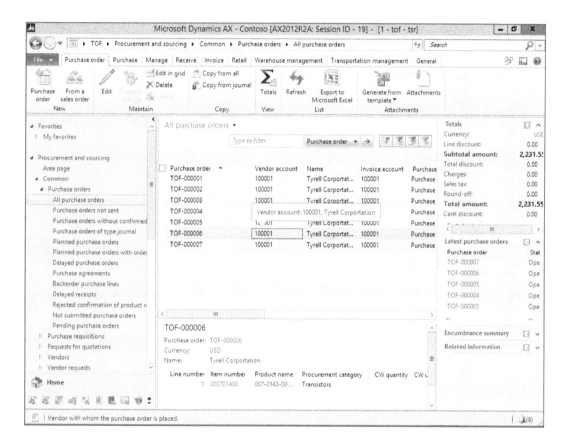

To see this in action, open up the **All Purchase Order** list page and click on the **Purchase Order** button within the **New** group of the **Purchase Order** ribbon bar.

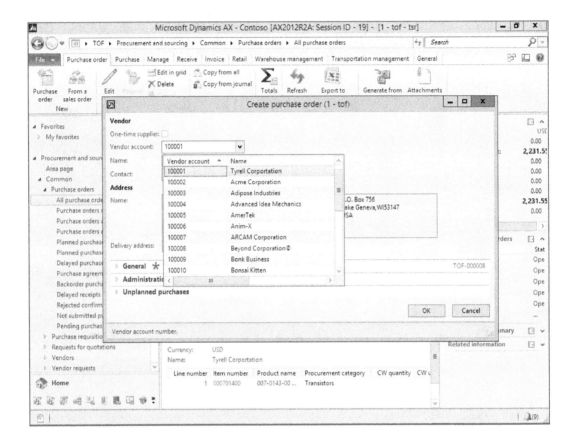

When the **Create Purchase Order** dialog box is displayed, click on the **Vendor Account** dropdown list and select the vendor that you want to create the Purchase Order for.

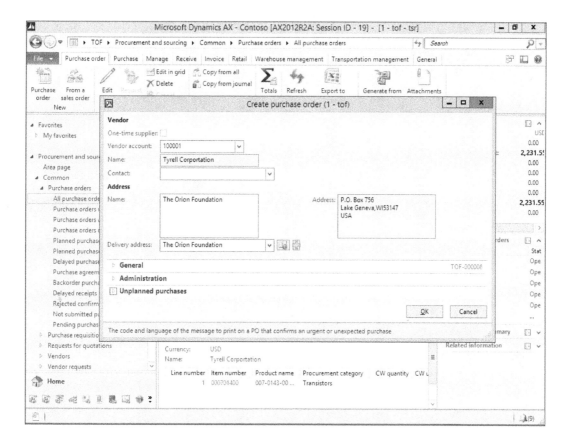

Then click on the **OK** button.

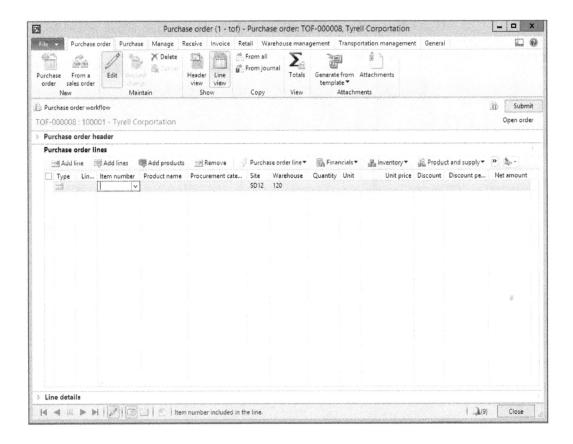

When the **Purchase Order Details** form is displayed, there will be a small change in the form of the workflow submission line will be shown.

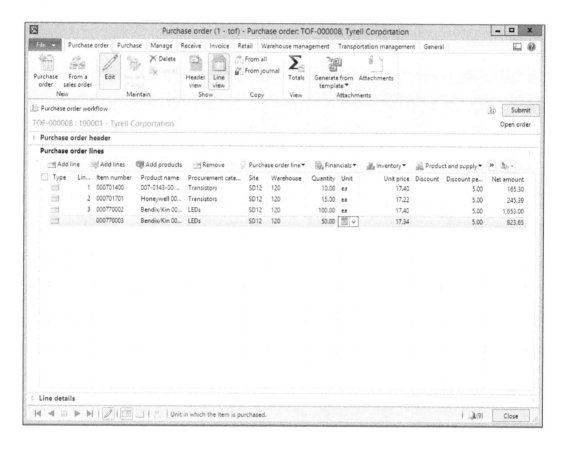

Before we submit the workflow though, add a few lines to the purchase order.

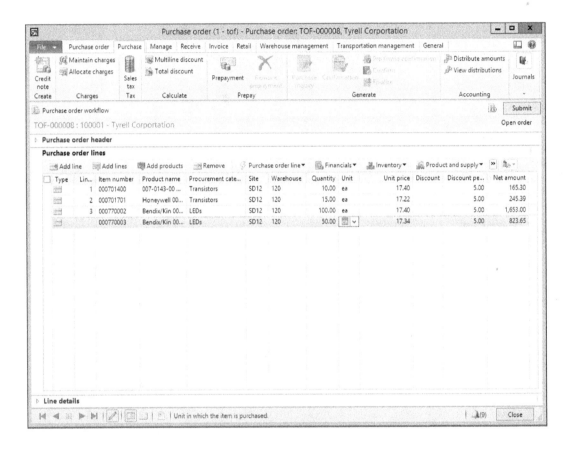

If you switch to the **Purchase** ribbon bar you will notice that you cannot Confirm the Purchase Order now – that is because you need to approve it first.

Enable Change Management On Purchase Orders To Track Changes

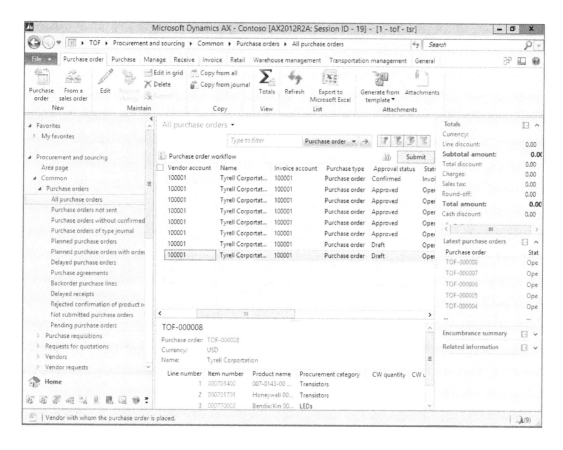

If you click on the **Close** button to exit out of the **Purchase Order** Details form then you will now notice that the Purchase Order has been set to a **Draft** approval status, and there is a submission option to send it to workflow for approval.

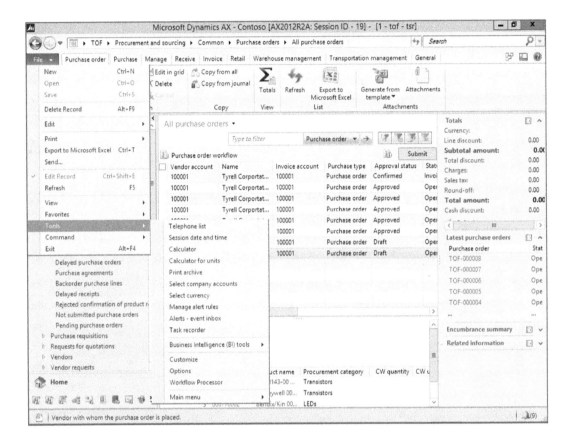

If you are running through these examples on the Demonstration Image, then you will probably need to start up the **Workflow Processor** at this time so that the workflows will be processed. To do this, click on the **File** menu, then click on the **Tools** submenu, and then select the **Workflow Processor** submenu item.

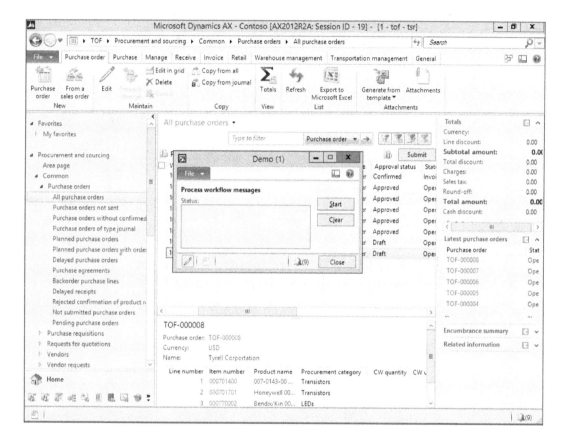

This will open up the **Demo Workflow Processor**.

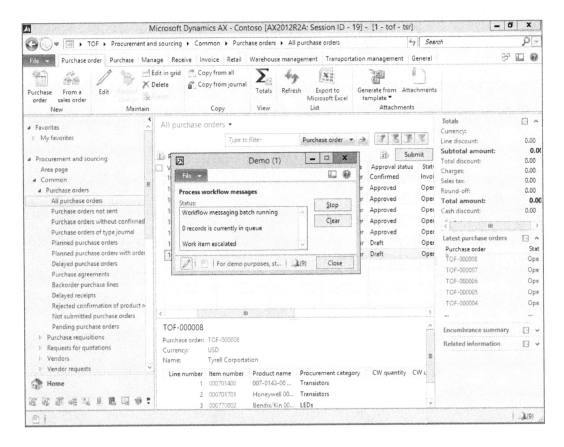

All you need to do is click on the **Start** button and then minimize the form.

Note: Don't close the form, because that will close the workflow processor.

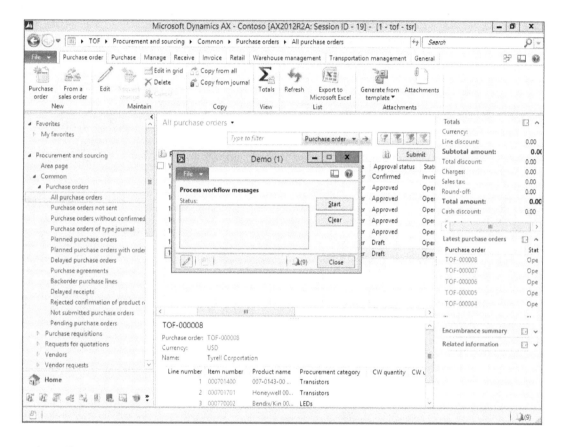

This will open up the **Demo Workflow Processor**.

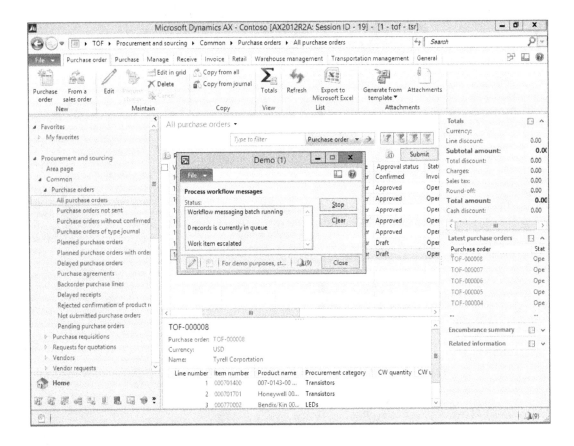

All you need to do is click on the **Start** button and then minimize the form.

Note: Don't close the form, because that will close the workflow processor.

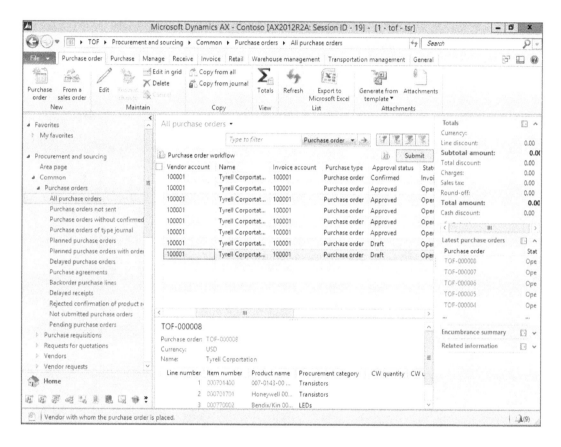

Now select the **Purchase Order** that you just created and click the **Submit** button to initiate the workflow process.

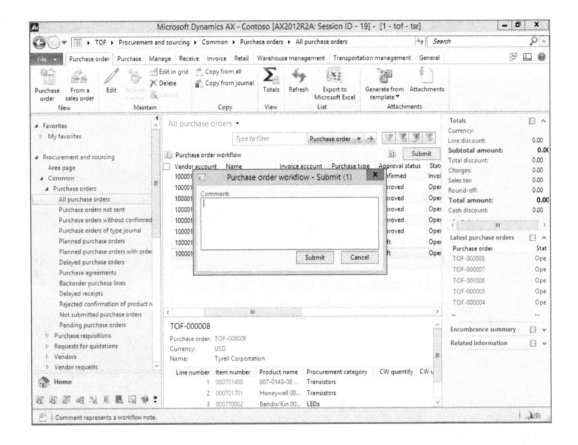

This will open up a **Comments** dialog box.

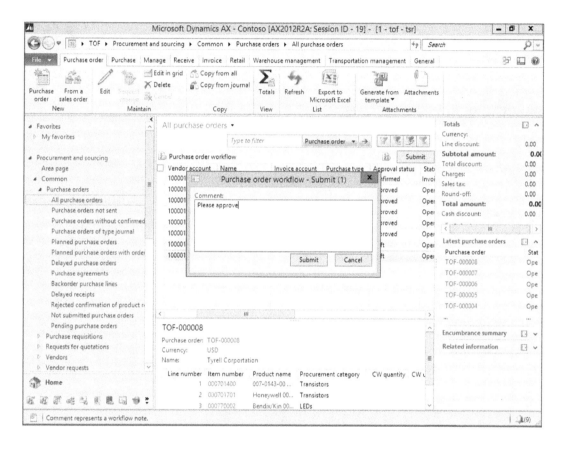

Enter in a quick note that will accompany the workflow and then click the **Submit** button.

Enable Change Management On Purchase Orders To Track Changes

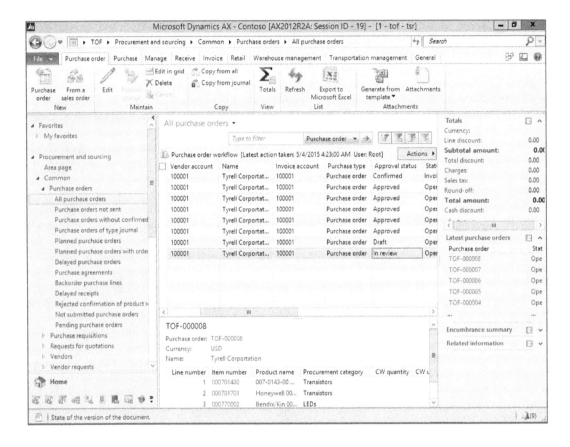

This will change the status of the purchase order to **In Review** and then allow you to approve the PO.

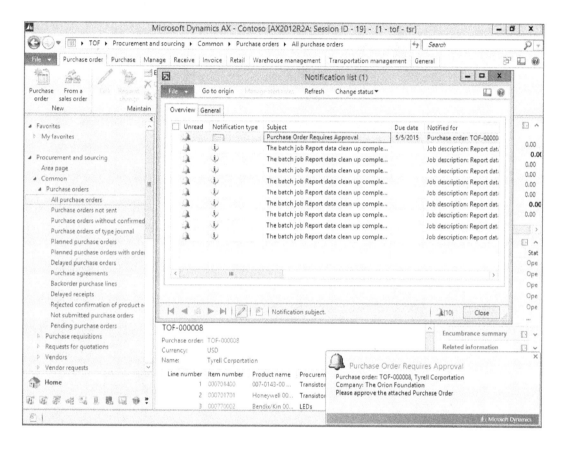

A few seconds later you should receive a notification that there is a **Purchase Order Approval** task that has been assigned to you. If you are impatient then you can also open up the **Notification List** and you will see the task there as well.

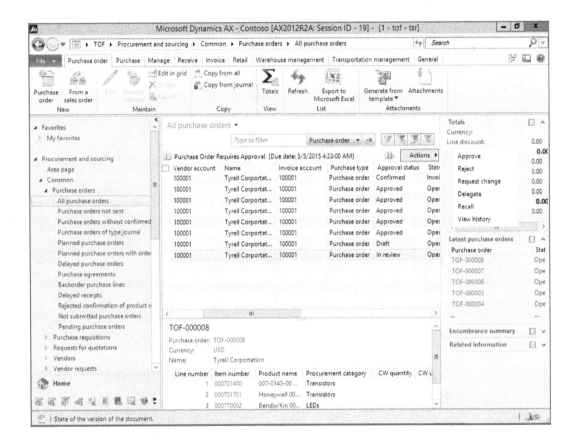

Return to the **All Purchase Orders** list page and if you click on the **Actions** button you will see that you can now route the **Purchase Order Approval**. Click on the **Approve** button to approve the Purchase Order.

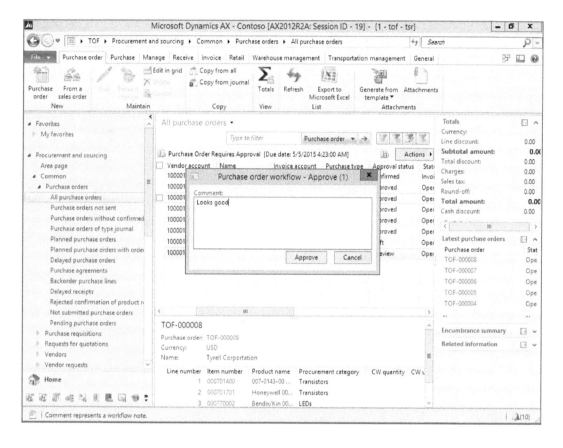

This will open up another **Comments** dialog where you can enter in a message and then click on the **Approve** button.

Enable Change Management On Purchase Orders To Track Changes

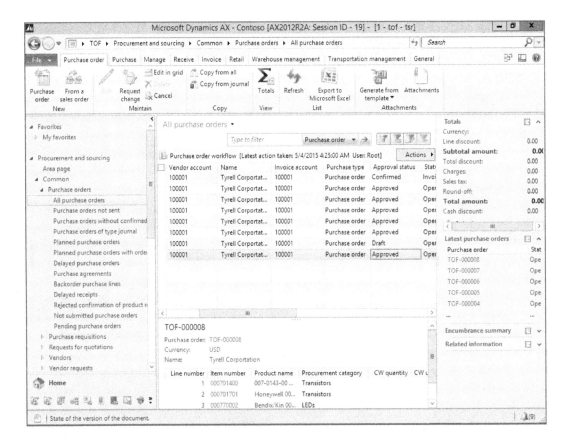

Once the **Purchase Order** is approved it will be given an **Approved** status and you will be able to send out the Purchase Order confirmation.

Requesting Changes To Purchase Orders

In addition to allowing you to approve Purchase Orders through workflows, the Change Management feature allows you to request and track changes to the purchase orders after they have been approved.

Enable Change Management On Purchase Orders To Track Changes

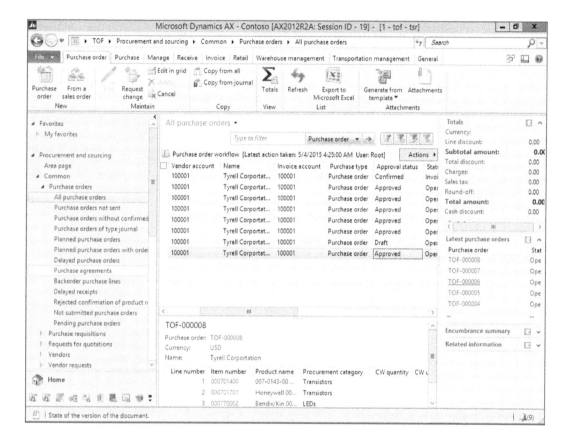

If you look at the **Purchase Order** ribbon bar, you will notice that the **Edit** option within the **Maintain** group is disabled, but the **Request Change** option is now enabled. To make an update to the **Purchase Order**, click on the **Request Change** button.

Enable Change Management On Purchase Orders To Track Changes

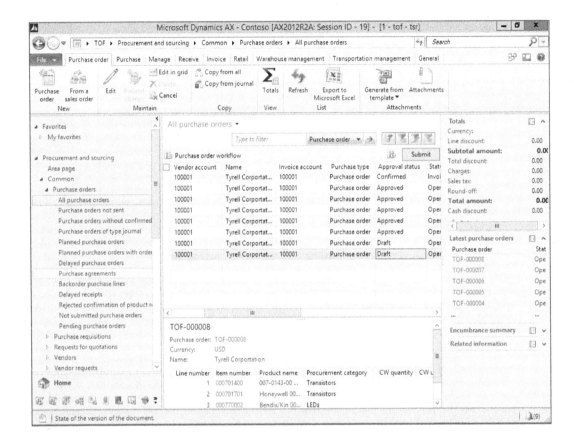

This will revert the **Purchase Order** back to a **Draft** approval status and the approval process needs to be completed before it is available to be sent out to the vendor again as a confirmation.

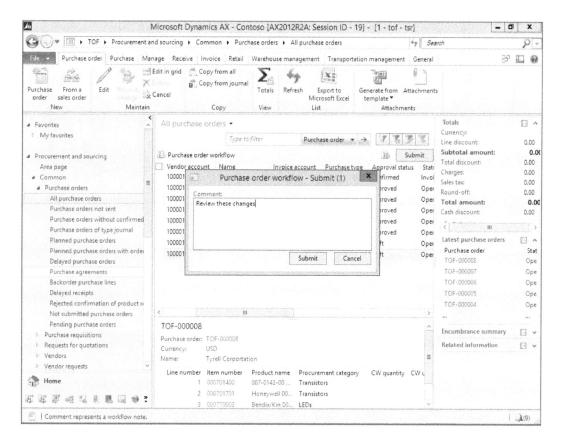

Now you can re-edit your **Purchase Order** and then resubmit it for approval by clicking on the **Submit** button in the header of the list page.

Viewing Change History

As a bonus, you can now track all of the versions of the **Purchase Orders**, view all of the changes that were made, and even compare **Purchase Orders** to see the differences.

Enable Change Management On Purchase Orders To Track Changes

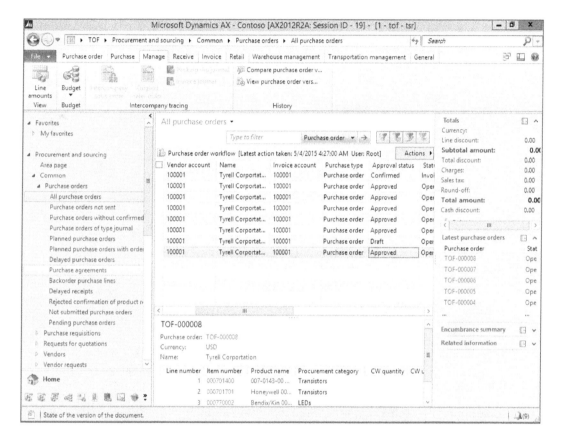

To view the different versions, click on the **View Purchase Order History** button within the **History** group of the **Manage** ribbon bar.

Enable Change Management On Purchase Orders To Track Changes

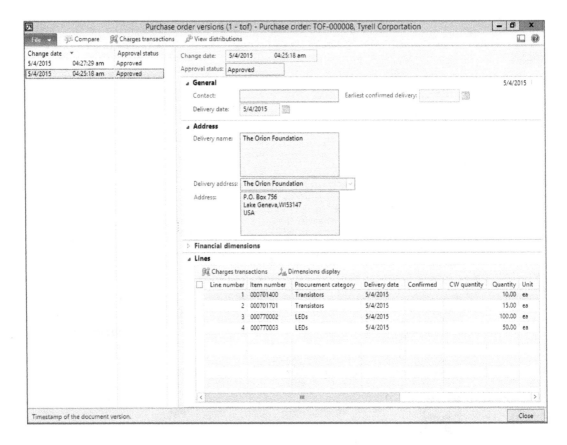

This will open up the **Purchase Order Versions** inquiry form and you will see all of the different version of the **Purchase Order**.

To see the changes made, click on the **Compare** button within the menu bar.

Enable Change Management On Purchase Orders To Track Changes

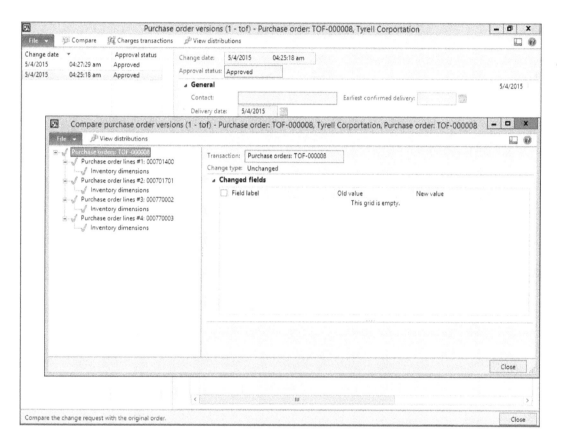

This will show you all of the changes between the two **Purchase Orders**.

When you are done comparing the versions, just click the **Close** button to exit from the form.

Enable Change Management On Purchase Orders To Track Changes

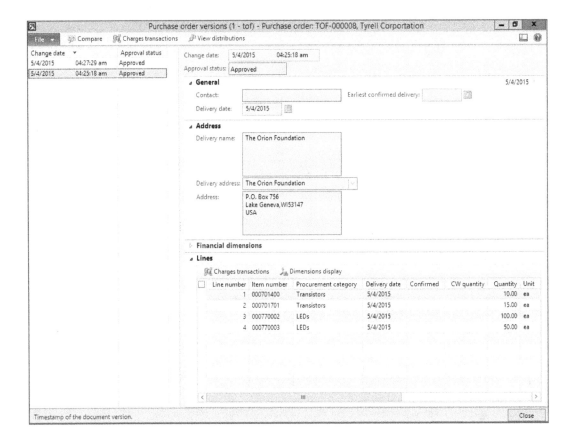

That will return you to the version history form, and when you are done here, just click on the **Close** button to exit from the history view.

SUMMARY

Hopefully this guide has given you a good foundation of knowledge of how the Procurement and Sourcing area of Dynamics AX works, and also some of the key features that are available for you that allow you to configure and manage your Purchase Orders.

We are still just starting you off on your journey through the Procurement and Sourcing module though. There is so much more that you can do including taking advantage of Requisitions, Requests for Quotation, Vendor Portal Management, Vendor Score Carding and even Vendor Onboarding, which we did not have space for in this guide. If you are interested in these topics then look for the second book that we will be releasing which will explain these more advanced features within the Procurement and Sourcing area of Dynamics AX.

Want More Tips & Tricks For Dynamics AX?

The Tips & Tricks series is a compilation of all the cool things that I have found that you can do within Dynamics AX, and are also the basis for my Tips & Tricks presentations that I have been giving for the AXUG, and online. Unfortunately book page size restrictions mean that I can only fit 50 tips & tricks per book, but I will create new volumes every time I reach the 50 Tip mark.

To get all of the details on this series, then here is the link:

http://dynamicsaxcompanions.com/tipsandtricks

daxc

Need More Help With Dynamics AX?

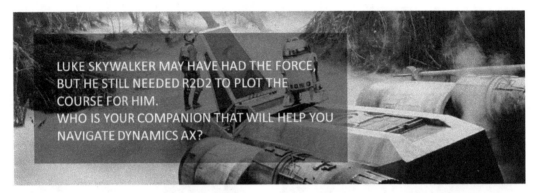

LUKE SKYWALKER MAY HAVE HAD THE FORCE,
BUT HE STILL NEEDED R2D2 TO PLOT THE
COURSE FOR HIM.
WHO IS YOUR COMPANION THAT WILL HELP YOU
NAVIGATE DYNAMICS AX?

After creating a number of my walkthroughs on SlideShare showing how to configure the different areas within Dynamics AX, I had a lot of requests for the original documents so that people could get a better view of many of the screen shots and also have a easy reference as they worked through the same process within their own systems. To make them easier to access, I am in the process of moving all of the content to the Dynamics AX Companions website to easier access. If you are looking for details on how to configure and use Dynamics AX, then this is a great place for you to start.

Here is the link for the site:

http://dynamicsaxcompanions.com/

About Me

I am an author - I'm no Dan Brown but my books do contain a lot of secret codes and symbols that help guide you through the mysteries of Dynamics AX.

I am a curator - gathering all of the information that I can about Dynamics AX and filing it away within the Dynamics AX Companions archives.

I am a pitchman - I am forever extolling the virtues of Dynamics AX to the unwashed masses convincing them that it is the best ERP system in the world.

I am a Microsoft MVP - this is a big deal, there are less than 10 Dynamics AX MVP's in the US, and less than 30 worldwide.

I am a programmer - I know enough to get around within code, although I leave the hard stuff to the experts so save you all from my uncommented style.

WEB	www.murrayfife.me www.dynamicsaxcompanions.com
EMAIL	murray@dynamicsaxcompanions.com
TWITTER	@murrayfife
SKYPE	murrayfife
AMAZON	www.amazon.com/author/murrayfife

www.ingramcontent.com/pod-product-compliance
Lightning Source LLC
Chambersburg PA
CBHW080143060326
40689CB00018B/3831